Mighty Optical Illusions

Mighty Optical Illusions

More Than 200 Images to Fascinate, Confuse, Intrigue, and Amaze

Steven Estep

Manager of MOillusions.com

Skyhorse Publishing

Skyhorse Publishing books may be purchased in bulk at special discounts for sales promotion, corporate gifts, fund-raising, or educational purposes. Special editions can also be created to specifications. For details, contact the Special Sales Department, Skyhorse Publishing, 307 West 36th Street, 11th Floor, New York, NY 10018 or info@skyhorsepublishing.com.

Skyhorse® and Skyhorse Publishing® are registered trademarks of Skyhorse Publishing, Inc.®, a Delaware corporation. Visit our website at www.skyhorsepublishing.com.

10 9 8 7 6 5 4 3 2 1

Library of Congress Cataloging-in-Publication Data is available on file.

Print ISBN: 978-1-63220-585-8

Printed in China

Table of Contents

Acknowledgments

I'd like to thank my grandmother, Margie Burdette, and my grandfather, Roy Burdette, who have treated me just like a child of their own, and still do. I love you both dearly.

My sister, Kristin Estep, who has always been there for me.

Of course, my loving and supportive girlfriend, Nicole Feliciani. You've always put up with me and my dreams, no matter how silly some of them may have been. I love you for that, and many other things, which would take an eternity to list. I will love you always.

I cannot express enough thanks to those illusionists out there who allowed me to feature their work in this book. I owe you all my gratitude and you've earned a friend for life.

Finally, I'd like to dedicate this book to my mother, Carla Taylor. I'll never forget how supportive you were of me and all my dreams. No matter what I did or wanted to do, you were always standing right behind me with nothing but words of encouragement. It didn't matter if I wanted to be a writer, filmmaker, musician, MMA fighter, or countless other things, you always told me I could do it and supported me 100 percent of the time.

Your love, positive energy, and spirit have been and always will be alive in me. You'll never know how greatly you impacted my life, and the lives of those around you. Therefore, this book is dedicated to you, Mom, because you always told me I could do it—and I did.

Introduction

My name is Steven Estep and I'm about to take you on a mind-blowing journey. You see, I'm a manager over at MOillusions.com, also known as Mighty Optical Illusions. Since my time there, I've encountered many amazing things. I've seen tons of images, text, and videos that have absolutely blown my mind. Also, the opportunity has allowed me to be in contact with some of the most brilliant minds I've ever had the pleasure to interact with. A lot of our submissions on the site come in from viewers, fans, readers, etc. Without these submissions, there's no way the site would be where it's at today. So, I can say without hesitation, all of this would not be possible without the fans of the website.

In addition to the fan submissions, I've had the unique pleasure of conversing with illusionists themselves, which has always been nothing less than spectacular. It seems a lot of people think that artists or illusionists would be extremely difficult to work with, but that has definitely not been the case. Of course, there are a couple exceptions here and there, but I can say that, for the most part, everyone has been an absolute pleasure to work with. Illusionists are some of the nicest and most easy-going people I have ever interacted with.

That being said, I must admit I was a bit nervous when contacting all of the illusionists on my contact list to see if they'd like to have their work featured in this book, but I found that most illusionists do not care about the money, fame, or anything of that nature. Instead, they just want to get their work in front of as many people as possible. They want to share their art with the world and, to me, that's a great thing.

I truly feel honored to bring you the illusions contained within the pages of this book. I've spoken with a ton of illusionists to make this happen and I can say with confidence that I have been able to bring together some of the greatest illusions ever created by some of the greatest illusionists the world has ever known. I've compiled it all into one book—the book that you're holding in your hands right now.

Now, as I said, I was able to get most of these illusions from the illusionists themselves. Some of the illusions were submissions, as I created a post on the website mentioning the upcoming book and that we were searching for illusions and illusionists to feature in the book. However, I did have to reach out and contact a ton of illusionists on my own, which, as I said, wasn't that difficult. Most illusionists were more than happy to hand over their work to be featured in the book.

As for the rest of the illusions, I was able to find both classic and modern illusions that were public domain and/or creative commons, which means I was allowed to use them freely in any type of media form. The public domain and creative commons images do not have the name of the illusionist underneath them. Unfortunately, I was not able to attain that information. As for the other illusions, I've listed the name of the creator under every single one. That way, they'll receive a bit of notoriety for being in the book and you'll also be able to easily look them up if you're a fan of their work.

As for the illusions you'll find in this book—I've tried my best to include a variety. In this book, you'll encounter illusions ranging from afterimages to scary illusions, and I've even tossed in some animated illusions, despite the fact that the images are obviously going to be static. So, without further ado, I'd like you to grab my hand and allow me to take you on this journey through the world of optical illusions. Buckle up, because it's going to be an amazing ride.

Steven Estep
10/09/2014
Beckley, West Virginia

Brain Teasers

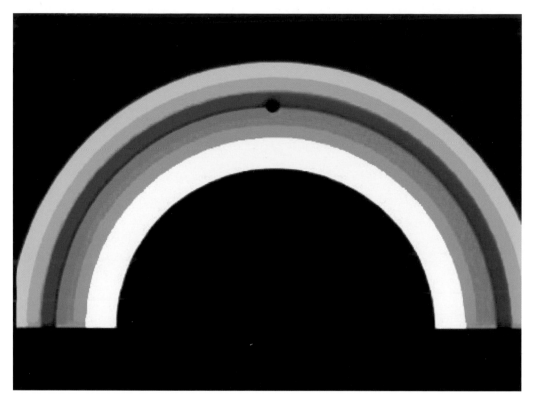

Illusion created by Steven Estep

Rainbow

Focus your vision on the black dot for 25 seconds.

Look at a solid surface, such as your ceiling or a wall.

Blink your eyes rapidly.

Enjoy!

Illusion created by Jennifer Townley

26.6 Days #1

2012 | 30 x 30 x 10 cm | Metal, wood, electric motor, mechanical parts, white cord, lead.

The four gears of this sculpture all have a different number of teeth, causing a change in composition after each rotation. The white cord that hangs from the gears exposes this compositional change. It forms a constantly changing quadrangle of which the amount of cord varies. It will display countless unique forms of the quadratical figure for a period of 26.6 days. Only then will the gears be in the initial composition and the cycle will start all over again.

Illusion created by Jennifer Townley

26.6 Days #2

2012 | 30 x 30 x 10 cm | Metal, wood, electric motor, mechanical parts, white cord, lead.

The four gears of this sculpture all have a different number of teeth, causing a change in composition after each rotation. The white cord that hangs from the gears exposes this compositional change. It forms a constantly changing quadrangle of which the amount of cord varies. It will display countless unique forms of the quadratical figure for a period of 26.6 days. Only then will the gears be in the initial composition and the cycle will start all over again.

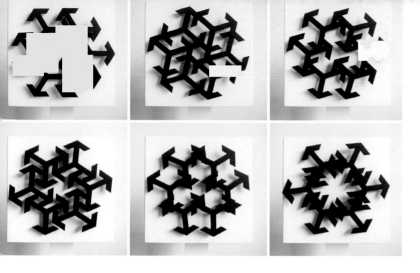

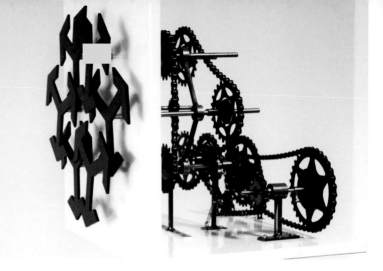

Illusions created by Jennifer Townley

Alhambra

2010 | 40 x 40 x 170 cm | Wood, steel, electric motor, mechanical parts.

This mechanical sculpture is based on a pattern drawn by M. C. Escher when he was at the Alhambra Palace in Spain. The pattern is built up from arrow-shaped figures, and by rotating these at different speeds and directions, brand new patterns emerge, all formed with the same basic shapes.

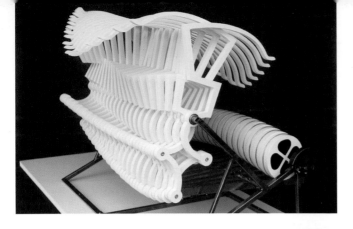
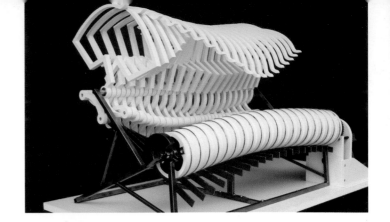
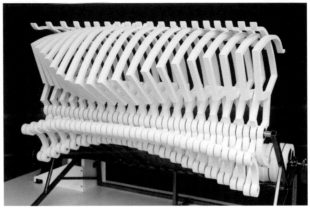

Illusions created by Jennifer Townley

Bussola

2014 | 120 x 60 x 70 cm | Wood, steel, mechanical parts, electric motor.

Bussola is named after the Italian word for *compass*, as this three-dimensional work is inspired by one of Leonardo da Vinci's designs for a compass dating back to 1514.

The machine consists of twenty identical elements whose mechanisms stick to the original design of the compass but whose form has somewhat been elaborated. They are built of four hinged parts, converting a vertical movement at the bottom hinge into a horizontal movement on the two upper legs. Driven by a camshaft, all the elements move in the same way, each with a small phase shift, creating a repetitive yet organic motion of the entirety. The assembled parts come across as one single moving form that behaves like a natural organism, a skeleton-like creature that seems to be traveling through space.

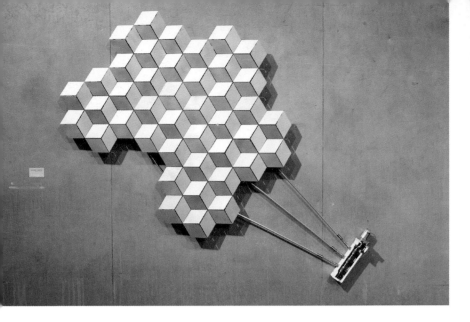 

Cubes

2013 | 160 x 180 x 12 cm | Aluminum, wood, steel, electric motor, mechanical parts.

This mechanical work is based on a geometric pattern of diamonds that creates the optical illusion of cubes, when in fact the cubes you see only consist of three diamond shaped aluminum plates grouped together.

Powered by a small electric motor and gear transmission, a mechanical construction at the back of the machine moves up and down very slowly. It tilts the aluminum plates back and forth, emphasizing the three dimensional form and therefore the illusion of the cubes. Because of the tilting, light is being reflected from various angles, which changes the color of the plates constantly. The perspective of the cubes keeps on changing; again and again the aluminum diamonds seem to connect themselves with a different cube.

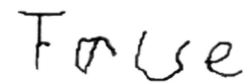

Illusion created by Steven Estep

True or False?

Now, you're probably wondering just what you're looking at in the above image. Well, that's the whole point of the optical illusion. This is a word illusion and it's your job to figure out what the word is that's being presented to you. Some people may say that the word is *True*, while others will say that the word is *False*, but I'm going to leave that up to you. Could you imagine putting this illusion to work in a real-life setting, such as a test paper at school? How would the teacher properly grade your paper? I guess it would depend on their perception. So, how do you perceive this illusion? Do you see *True*, or *False*?

Hidden Optical Illusions

Illusion created by Mark Talbot

Australia

In the above illustration, you'll see a rendition of a popular Australian setting overlooking Ulu-ru, which is also known as Ayres Rock. However, there's something hidden in the image above and I would like for you all to be able to figure it out on your own. The above image was created with a lot of attention to detail in order to achieve the desired effect. Are you able to find the hidden image? Do you give up? If so, keep reading and you'll find the answer below.

The user submitted this image, because he believed that a lot of optical illusions are created in the United States and/or Europe, so this would give the book a nice international feel. Without a doubt, he was able to achieve what he wanted with this illusion.

ANSWER: Hidden within the trees, you'll see the map of Australia.

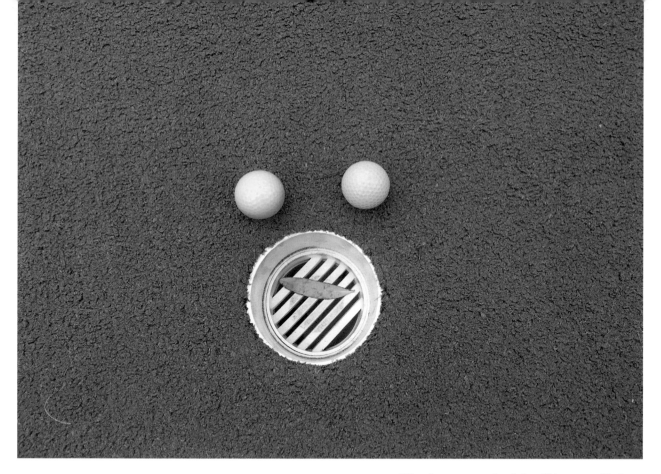

Golf Ball Face

This optical illusion serves as a reminder that illusions can be found anytime, anywhere. I was on vacation with my girlfriend when we decided to play some miniature golf. On one particular hole, we both came very close with our shots, but didn't quite make it in the hole, as you can see in this picture. I realized that the end effect was what looked like a cartoonish face, so I took a quick snapshot before resuming our game.

Yes, I know this illusion is a bit silly, but that's the whole point. I just hope this image was able to make you crack a smile or laugh, rather than rolling your eyes.

Hidden Faces in Mountains

Some of my favorite illusions I come across are the ones where you have to spot the hidden object. I find that these particular illusions are among some of the most challenging, which makes the whole experience for the viewer much more enjoyable. There are hidden faces in the image above and it's your job to spot them, but it's going to be a bit difficult, as the faces are hidden among the terrain.

Illusion created by Steven Estep

Owl

Illusions can be found anywhere, anytime. Sometimes, the illusions can be found in places you least expect them, as they become a part of something that you're so used to seeing. For instance, have you ever just gotten a fresh, hot cup of coffee, started to take a drink, and then you see a face staring right back at you? In this optical illusion image, it seems as if you can see an animal in this cup off of coffee. Can you guess what animal is staring back at you?

This illusion was digitally manipulated to achieve the effect you see above, but there have been many instances in which people have seen what appears to be a face or eyes in their coffee. Make sure you look at your coffee the next time you get yourself a cup, rather than mindlessly taking a drink. You never know, you might just find yourself staring at an optical illusion.

Pasta Face

Cooking can be a daunting task, depending on the person you ask, but I've always found that cooking presents a great opportunity to discover optical illusions. In years of viewing optical illusions, I've seen a ton of them that involve food. Sure, some of them have been deliberately created by the chef, while others were discovered totally by accident. As you can see in the image above, there appears to be a face that has formed in a pot of boiling pasta, which serves to remind us that optical illusions are always popping up all around us. If you're an observant person that tries to remain aware of your surroundings, you'll be amazed at how many illusions you will stumble across.

Illusion created by Terence Rosoman

Dot Art

The dots in this optical illusion are camouflaging a very popular piece of artwork.

Can you figure out what's hidden behind them?

Hint: Move the book further away from your face, and the image will begin to reveal itself.

Illusion created by Terence Rosoman

Secret Message

Here we have another piece of work from Terence Rosoman, which is very similar to his other piece that's featured in this book. However, instead of a picture being hidden, this time you'll find hidden text. Now, I have to warn you, if you're part of our younger audience, you may want to move on to a different illusion in the book, as this illusion does contain adult language. Even though this illusion contains some adult language, you can't deny that it's an amazing piece of work.

Having trouble seeing the illusion? Move the book a bit further from your face and the text will slowly begin to reveal itself.

Optical illusions are a lot of fun, because they can be a game where people have to find hidden people, animals, or in this case, a face at the top of the hill. The human eyes and the human brain together are like the world's most sophisticated computer that can pick up things like the images in this optical illusion. The first thing that people are going to see is the face at the top of the hill. If people look closely, they can see how this remarkable illusion was accomplished.

The small bushes along the sides of the hill make up both the hair and the beard of the figure. A small set of stairs at the bottom of the hill makes up the figure's ear, and a hole in the direct center of the hill is the figure's eye. If people are having problems seeing the face at the top of the hill, all they have to do is turn their head to the side and the image will become clear.

A fun way to do an optical illusion is to have a hidden image within another image. The above image is clearly a face, but the wood "liar" is also embedded into this face. The use of the wording is very clever, because the word itself is what actually does create the face. The letter L in the word "liar" is what makes up the eyes and the glasses that are covering them.

The nose in the face is created by the cursive letter I, which then goes to the mouth. The lips and mouth are created by the letter A, which then goes to the letter R that creates the chin. For those people that are having a hard time seeing the word "liar," the best way to see it is to turn the head or rotate the image sideways.

Music is important to a lot of people, especially those that have worked long and hard in order to play a musical instrument. For those that love the saxophone, the above image appears to be the black silhouette of a saxophone player, but there is more than one image associated with this optical illusion. If people take a closer look at the black silhouette saxophone player, another image can be seen.

Part of the saxophone player makes up a second image of a young woman. For those people that need a hint, because they cannot see the young woman, the eye, nose, and lips of the woman can easily be seen. The bottom of the young woman's face is created by the saxophone player's instrument, which then creates her chin and neck.

Many artists like to include some kind of hidden image when they are creating a great work of art. At first glance, the above optical illusion looks like a man wearing a sombrero, a pink colored shirt, and riding on top of a white horse. The image also shows that the man on the horse is riding by a river. There is also a man lying on the ground near the shore of the river covered up with a yellow blanket. The man on the horse is riding under a brick bridge.

If people look closely enough, they will see that the man on the horse, combined with the other aspects of the picture, form a hidden old man. The hidden old man has long white hair and a white beard. The man on the horse creates the eyes, the nose, and mouth of the old man.

Optical illusions can happen anywhere, even in the middle of the woods. The above photo was taken while a herd of deer were wandering around the woods. For those people that are having a hard time seeing the deer, the best place to spot them is to look along the center of the photo. The color of the deer's hides is just the right shade of tan to really blend into the trees and the leaf-covered ground.

In order to create this illusion, the photographer had to be very patient because the deer might not come around too often unless they are hungry. Deer are also very sensitive to the presence of human beings. The photographer who took this picture had to stand a distance away to make sure that he or she was not disturbing the deer and would not frighten them away before the photograph could be taken.

People often love to take photographs of mountains, especially when they are covered in snow. Sometimes people can take pictures, but do not realize that they have actually taken a photograph that contains an optical illusion. In the above photograph, there is snow all over the mountain. If you look closely, you will see an image located in the center of the photograph. The snow on the mountain is beginning to melt, which is causing all kinds of unique images.

There is an angel located on the mountain with her wings spread. However, the angel is not alone because there is also another image located right beside her. To the left of the spread winged angel, there is a triangle-headed monster that has an evil sneer on its face. The angel better watch out and fly away fast, or the monster of the mountain may come after her.

The two colors of black and white are the two most contrasting colors there are, which makes them perfect when it comes to creating optical illusions. At first glance at the image above, people are going to see either two faces looking at one another or a black chalice in the middle of the image. For those that are having a hard time seeing the faces, all they have to do is look toward the center at the thinnest part of the chalice.

What creates the tiniest part of the chalice is a pair of noses. Once people see the noses, the rest of the faces should easily be seen, including the mouths, the slopes of the forehead, and the chins. However, some people are going to see chalice first because it is the stronger of the two colors, which means it will attract the eyes before the faces do.

At first glance, the posted image above looks like a duck with a slightly open beak. However, other people may disagree with the first image that can be seen and claim that they see a rabbit with its ears laid back. The people that claim to see the rabbit will point out that the rabbit is complete, including the fact that it has a nose. For those that see the duck, the first thing they will point out is the fact that there is an imperfection with the head. The best way to see the rabbit clearly is to turn the image to the side, which will be a lot easier than having to strain the neck by turning the head to one side.

Some people may not see the word "illusion" first because their eye is naturally drawn to the white that the image contains. While people are busy looking at the two words "optical" and "illusion," they may not even see that the word "illusion" actually has a nice picturesque scene in it. If people look closely they will see a beautiful blue sky, a lovely field, and mountain in the distance.

The Grand Canyon is located in the state of Arizona. The Grand Canyon was created by water, and some of the shapes that are within it are quite remarkable. Millions of people travel to the Grand Canyon, and pay a lot of money to tour its interior on foot or even on the back of a donkey. In the above image, a group of tourists are standing on the top of the canyon looking down into it, but there is more than just the five people that are touring it. To the right of the people standing on the top of the canyon, there is an optical illusion that looks just like a sixth member of the group.

Watching the beautiful ocean moving, and the waves crashing on the rocks, is something very relaxing that people often like to do. There are seven oceans located around the globe, but not everyone lives close enough to see one of them. The ocean is so popular that people who live too far from it will do absolutely anything to see it, including traveling hundreds of miles away from home just to walk on the wet sand or dip their toes in the ocean.

In the above image, there are two rock formations that are facing the swirling ocean. If people look close enough, they will see that there are ridges along the edge of the two rocks that look just like faces. Even the rocks want to watch the ocean, and in this image, that is exactly what they are doing.

The above image is a picture of a soldier in his camouflage. Some people may not notice the soldier right away because his camouflage is so good that he blends in with the trees and forest all around him. Can you spot the soldier? Time yourself and see how long it takes you.

The above picture is a fine example of seeing a face in an unusual item. The door hinge may look old and rusty, but it also looks happy, because the screws look like eyes, the middle hole looks like a nose, and the half circle shape looks exactly like a smiling mouth. This image just goes to show that even in the worst situations, a rusty old hinge can still keep a positive attitude and be happy.

Sometimes when people look at things, like a row of columns, the lights and shadows can play tricks on the eyes. The most innocent things, like columns in a building, can actually look like something else if things are observed from a certain point of view. When people look at the above picture of a row of bright yellow columns, they may see the columns, or they may actually see a row of men standing together facing one another.

Some may see the people first, and the columns second, but it also depends on how good of an imagination they have. Whether or not the men in the above image exist is a question that truly has no answer. People can decide for themselves whether the picture above is a row of men or just a row of columns mixed in with a few dark shadows.

Impossible Optical Illusions

Illusion created by Frankynata Tedjosantoso

Plane

The above illusion appears at the Guangzhou airport. As you can see, it looks as if there's a transparent ramp that is leading to an airplane, which, despite the transparency, is totally normal. Actually, there was no airplane at the ramp in the above picture. Instead, the airplane is being reflected by a mirror in the airport, which gives off the illusionary effect you see above. Luckily, a picture was taken at the right moment, with the right angle, to capture the amazing results you see in the picture.

Illusion created by Josh Stacy

Cards

If you were in need of a deck of cards, you'd be in for a rude awakening, as this deck of cards seems to be trapped inside of a bottle and there's no way to get it out other than breaking the bottle. Josh Stacy has managed to trap an object inside of a bottle that would be impossible to pass through the mouth of the bottle. So, how was he able to accomplish such an illusion? It would be safe to assume that he used a glass blowing technique to make the mouth of the bottle larger, inserted the deck of cards and then closed it back up, which gives the effect you see above.

Need a Light?

Josh Stacy is an optical illusionist that specializes in impossible bottles and the like. I guess for this illusion, you would call it an impossible light bulb. As you can see, Mr. Stacy has replaced the inner-workings of a light bulb with a small box of matches. If you need a light, you won't be able to plug this light bulb into a socket. Instead, you'll have to resort to using the matches inside of the light bulb, but how could you possibly get to those matches without breaking the glass?

How was the illusionist able to get the matches in the light bulb without breaking it? After all, the opening is much too small for a box of matches to pass through it, as you will be able to see in the picture on the next page.

So, how was this illusion accomplished?

As for this illusion in particular, it was likely accomplished by using a glass blowing technique. The object was placed in the bulb and then the opening was heated until it was molten hot. At that point, it was likely the neck was reshaped to be narrower and the mouth was made smaller, thus giving us the effect we see in the pictures.

Illusion created by Josh Stacy

Locked Cards

This is very similar to the other card illusion that Josh Stacy created, in which an entire deck of cards is trapped within the confines of a glass bottle. However, this time he decided to take his illusion a bit further and trap a deck of cards inside of a bottle, as well as put a lock on top of the cards. Of course, neither of the objects inside of the bottle would be small enough to fit through the mouth of the bottle, so it's likely he accomplished this illusion by employing a glass blowing technique.

Woodwork

The image above plays on your sense of perception. Are the two blocks in the image above side-by-side or are they on top of each other? It actually looks like both, so how was this mind-boggling illusion pulled off? Most people immediately jump to the conclusion that this type of illusion was accomplished with photo-editing software, such as Photoshop, but this one wasn't.

The image you're seeing above is real wood and wasn't manipulated digitally in any way, shape, or form. Also, there aren't two blocks of wood in the image above. Instead, it's just a single block of wood with some simple cuts in it and some lines that were drawn on it to give it a 3D effect.

Illusion created by Josh Stacy

Master Lock

Josh Stacy is a master when it comes to getting objects inside of bottles that would be absolutely impossible for them to pass through the opening in the bottle. This time, he's inserted multiple locks inside of a bottle and also connected them to a chain. As you can see, there's a lock on the top of the bottle, showing that there's no way these locks would ordinarily be able to make it inside the bottle, but a couple of them did. It's likely that a glass blowing technique was used to make the opening of the bottle wider until he was able to put the objects inside and then he shrunk it back down to its original size.

Illusion created by Josh Stacy

Wooden Bolt

Once again, Josh Stacy has managed to fit an object inside of a bottle that normally would not be able to pass through the opening of the bottle. This time, he has a long piece of wood going into the bottle, which would normally fit, but there's a bolt on the end of the wood, which would not be able to fit through the opening in the bottle. It's likely that a glass blowing technique was used in order to accomplish an illusion of this caliber.

Squares

2014 | 110 x 110 x 25 cm | Wood, aluminum, electric motor and mechanical parts.

Four white gears positioned in a square make the mechanical base of this simple but effective moving sculpture. On the edge of the gears, there are two identical overlapping black grids connected and one grid is attached to two gears. The grids only consist of squares, but when they start to move their forms merge into new patterns. Small and big squares and rectangles are constantly changing shape, direction and position. As some squares grow, others get smaller, all perfectly balanced.

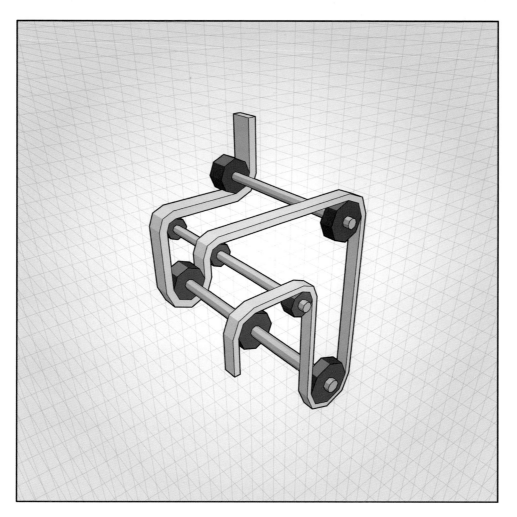

Illusion created by Andreas Aronsson

Belt

My original sketch for this figure was a bit simpler, with just five wheels, but while I was drawing it on the computer I added one wheel to the sketch. But after finishing that version of the figure I decided to add another two wheels, just because they fit. And I think that made it into an interesting piece of art.

The belt goes back and forth between the different axles, but as it does that it also travels forward and backward while only bending around one axis. —Andreas Aronsson

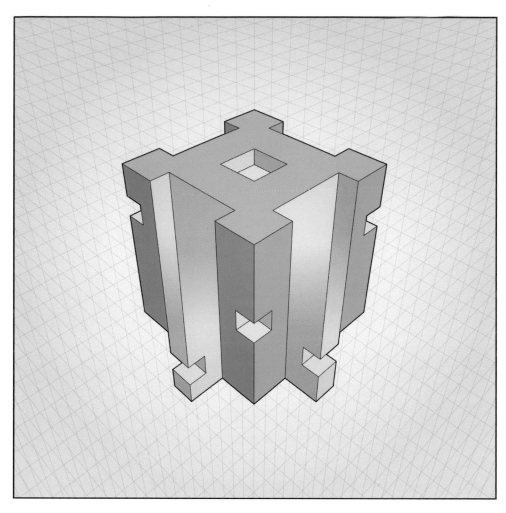

Illusion created by Andreas Aronsson

Block

I tend to not make many pieces where surfaces change direction or vanish, mostly because it's harder to imagine and then harder to color. But with that, they are also more satisfying to finish, so I guess it works both ways!

From the bottom, the middle column on each side turns to spacing between two other columns at the top. —Andreas Aronsson

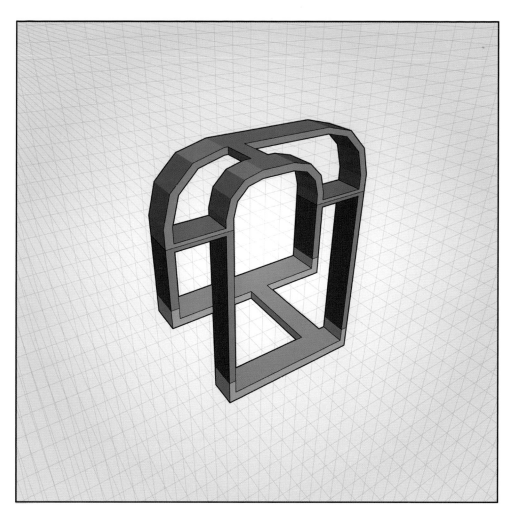

Illusion created by Andreas Aronsson

Building

There is a wide roof and a deep floor, but at the same time all the walls are connected horizontally. —Andreas Aronsson

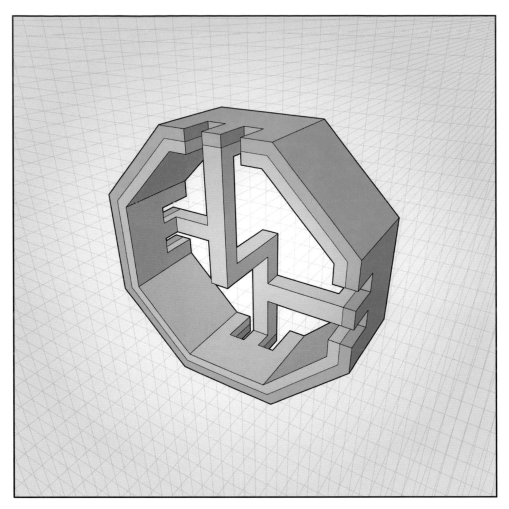

Illusion created by Andreas Aronsson

Circle

I was going for an easy one because my schedule around Christmas and New Year was super busy, but as I was pretty tired the progress was really slow, and I eventually complicated it a whole lot so it was not very easy anyway!

In this figure, you can travel from the back to the front even if you only walk sideways. There is also a distance between back and back, and front and front, while they are all connected in the center. —Andreas Aronsson

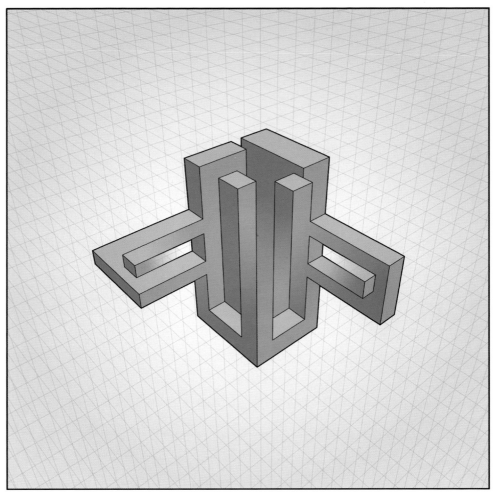

Complex

This is one of the impossible figures that I myself feel works a bit better as just linework. This might be because the figure looks bent with the gradients, so the lines-only version looks cleaner, which is without saying, really. Still, colors give volume and make things look nice.

Both the tower and the wings transform from one end to the other. What was in front goes behind, what was a solid turns into air, surfaces from different structures melt into a new single one. —Andreas Aronsson

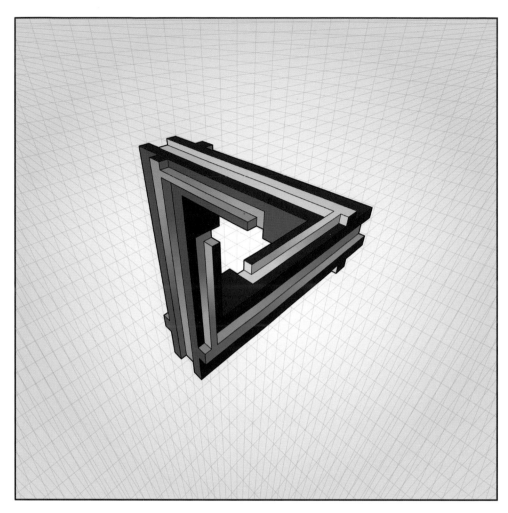

Illusion created by Andreas Aronsson

Tribar

On this impossible tribar, there are also ridges that turn inside out, twice! —Andreas Aronsson

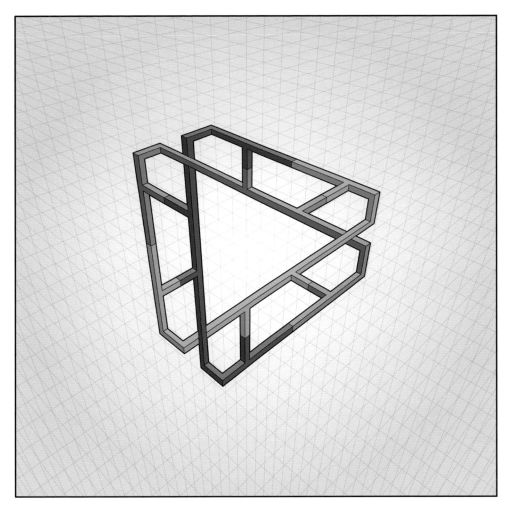

Illusion created by Andreas Aronsson

Double Tribar

A large impossible tribar contains a smaller one, connected on all sides. —Andreas Aronsson

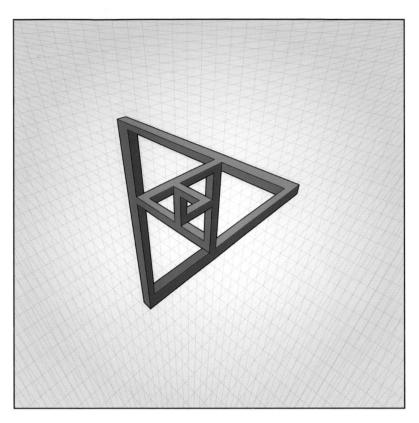

Illusion created by Andreas Aronsson

Triple Tribar

You can travel infinitely in any direction by walking through this figure. As it was drawn with an equal distance between all vanishing points, as I have been doing for a while now, some interesting geometrical things happened. I tried to find where on the outer tribar the inner should be anchored, and while plotting several inner tribars I tried to figure out some kind of relationship.

What I finally found was that the intersections of the lines for the outside of the inner tribars all lined up on a circle. To my surprise, this circle had the exact same size as a circle crossing through all vanishing points, and it would intersect the center of the tribars which was what I looked for. It also crossed through the absolute center of the vanishing points! Phew! —Andreas Aronsson

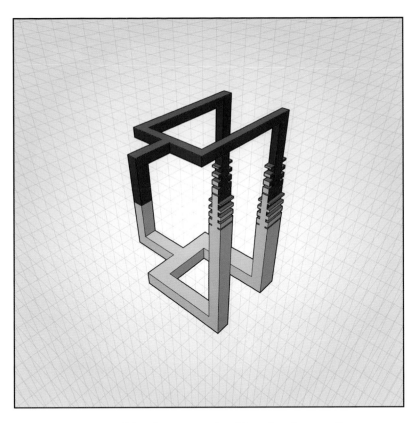

Illusion created by Andreas Aronsson

Forks

The day after I had finished this one, having spent a lot of time thinking about the design, I decided to redo it. I was unhappy with how it looked and I quickly decided what to change, but it required almost a complete remake. In total, I've probably spent more than eight hours on drawing in perspective… I'll try to make another progress composite with all my reference lines visible; there is no automatic process, though, so I need to take 60+ screen grabs and blend them in Photoshop.

The two forks are connected at both ends while being perpendicular to each other.
—Andreas Aronsson

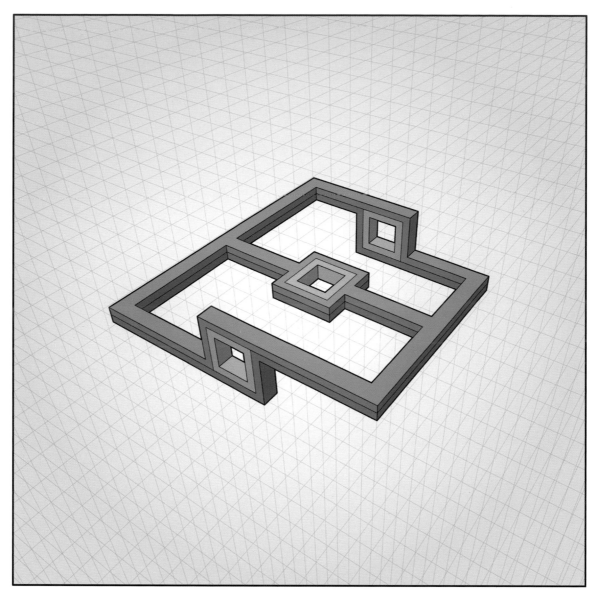

Hoops

Travel clockwise and you will only go downward, anticlockwise and you will go upwards.
Meanwhile the center makes it all flat. —Andreas Aronsson

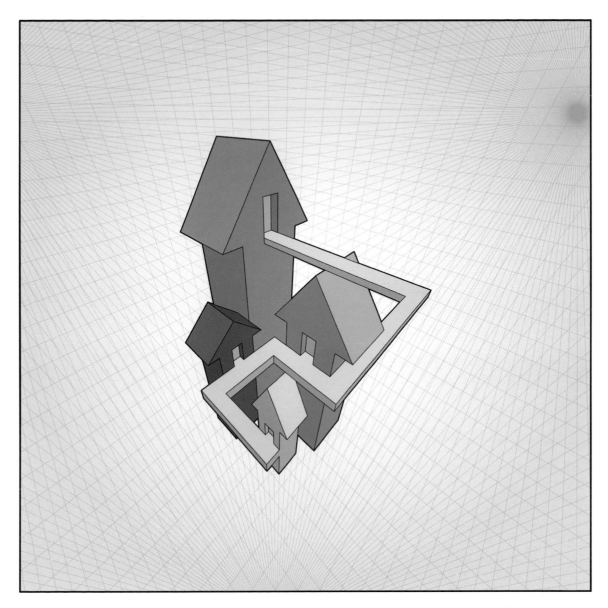

Hus

Even though the houses are of different heights, the gangway, which is perfectly horizontal, connects all the entrances. —Andreas Aronsson

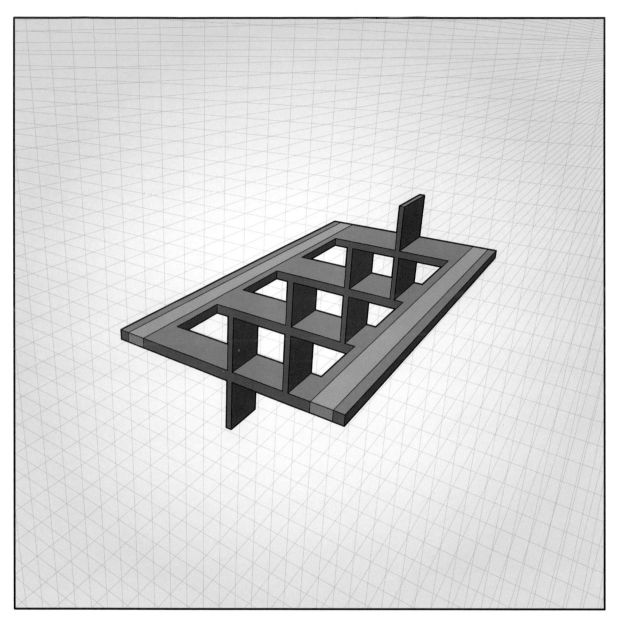

Lattice

In between the tracks, there are also vertical boards connecting the horizontal beams. This way, you can travel from the first to the last beam both horizontally and vertically.

—Andreas Aronsson

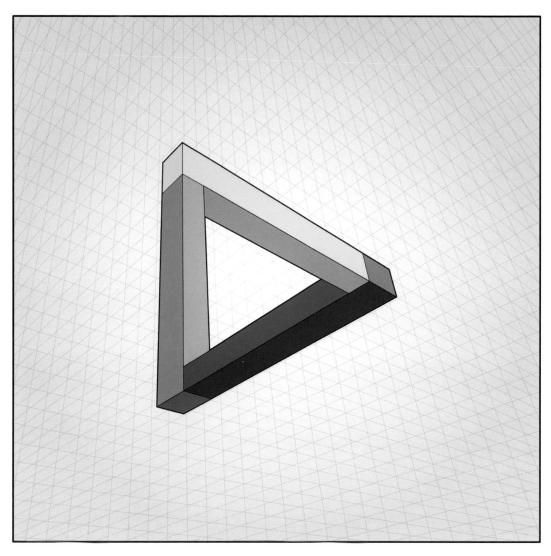

Penrose

This is probably the first illusion I have created where I started out directly in CAD with no base model created in 3D first. I had to figure out how to place my perspective points, and the eventual and fairly obvious answer in this case was to use the corners of a like-sided triangle.

The three rectangular bars are placed in 3D space in such a way that the front end of one connects to the back end of another. This way, you can travel continuously back into the picture or forward out of the picture by tracing the shape. —Andreas Aronsson

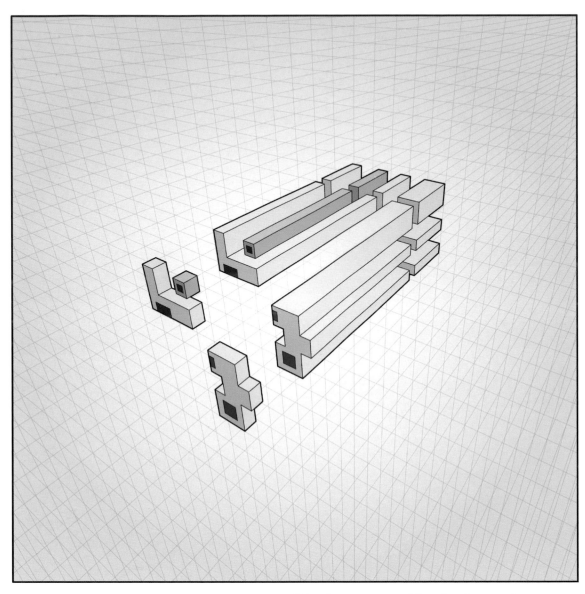

Illusion created by Andreas Aronsson

Rocket

From the right to the left, six bars turn into one bar and two shapes. —Andreas Aronsson

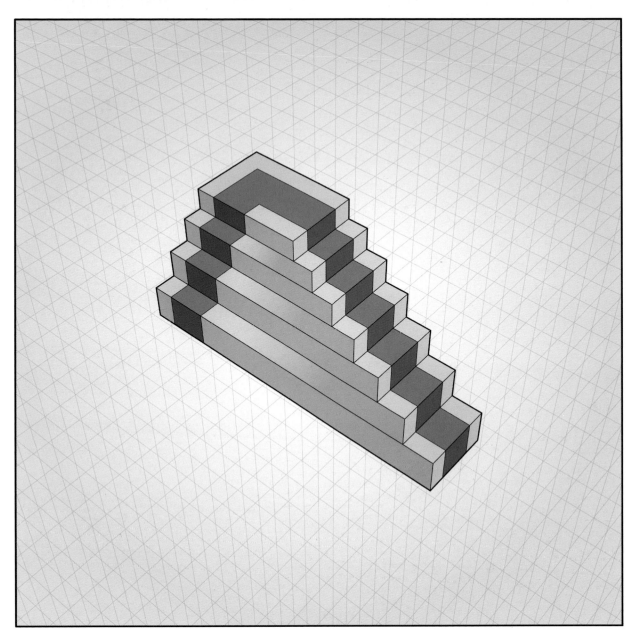

Illusion created by Andreas Aronsson

Stairs

Depending on which side you access this pair of stairs, you get to climb a different number of steps. —Andreas Aronsson

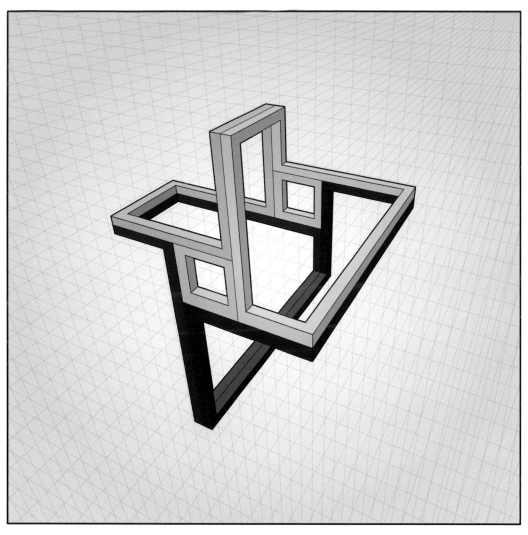

Illusion created by Andreas Aronsson

Stars

After I had finished this one, I realized I could make it even more impossible by simply putting things that should be in front behind instead. Then I remembered my conclusion from half a decade ago, that too many impossibilities together just becomes confusing, it's often better to focus on once concept. Unless, of course, confusion is what you want.

Two sides are mirrored versions of each other but still connected as if they were symmetrical. —Andreas Aronsson

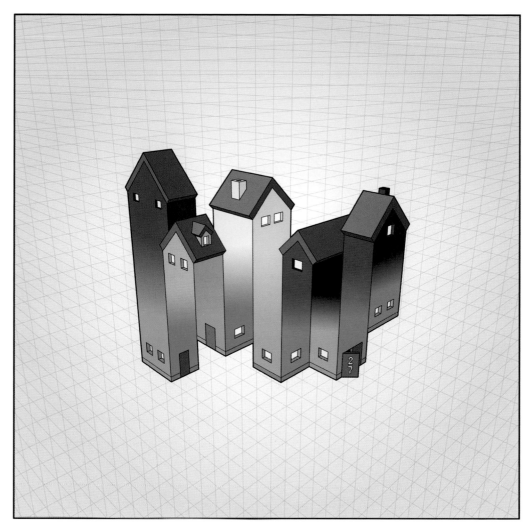

Illusion created by Andreas Aronsson

Town

Which way are the walls facing? How many houses are there? Depending on where you look, you will get different answers! —Andreas Aronsson

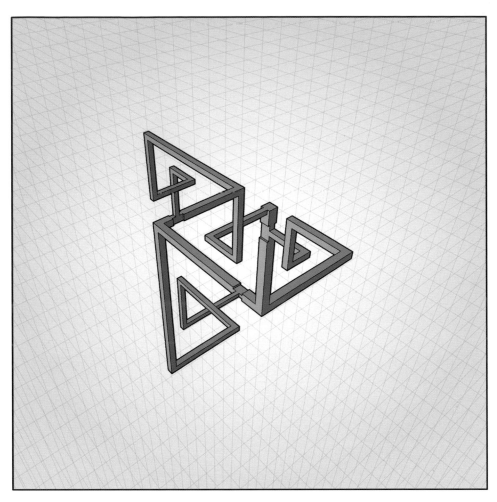

Illusion created by Andreas Aronsson

Triangle

It took me quite a while to decide how to start the work on this figure. It felt a bit too daunting in the beginning when I tried to create the initial geometry out of a bunch of floating bars, but I settled for a simpler and actually better method to realize it. As it is fairly complex, it was hard to write any explanatory text, but I guess it does not really need that.

The general shape of this figure is a triangle, but it is more intricate than that. It is actually a double tribar with another three double tribars attached to it, making it a quad-double tribar! —Andreas Aronsson

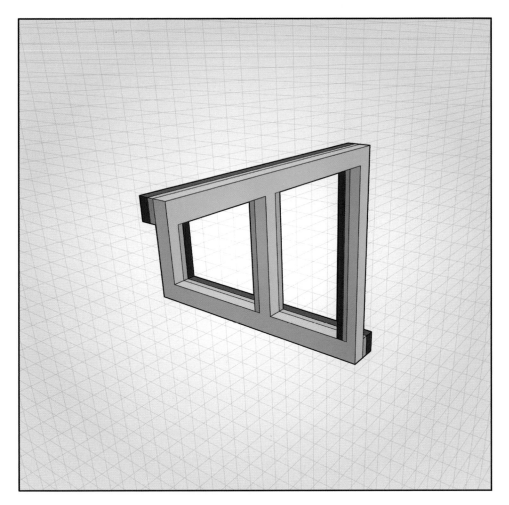

Trident

The green part of the figure is taller on the right side than the left, while still being a single object. The colored parts show the conflicting differences in width due to perspective distortion.

—Andreas Aronsson

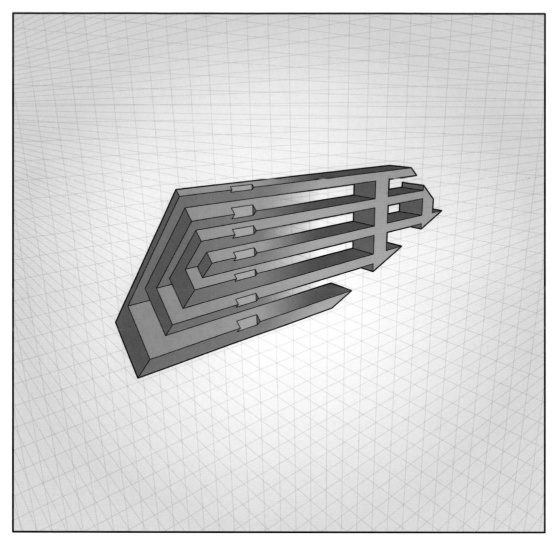

Illusion created by Andreas Aronsson

Wave

The left and right sides are very different, even if it's one object. The general structure is rotated, surfaces turns into void, depths turn flat. Also notice that the right side has been cut so it would appear like the shape of the left side continues all the way. And on the left side there are cuts that appear to be connected. —Andreas Aronsson

People travel around the world to check out all of its natural wonders, which may include a natural setting with a beautiful waterfall. This optical illusion involves a natural setting, a waterfall, and a plastic bottle of water. In order to create this illusion, the photographer, and the man with the bottle of water, have to be standing in just the right place.

Once again, this optical illusion is all about the timing of the pouring water and how it blends into the waterfall. Also, the position of the bottle has to be just right because if the bottle is too high or too low, the photograph will not come out right. The camera also has to be placed just the right way, at just the right distance, so that the background contains the waterfall and the pouring bottle that creates the illusion.

There are many phenomena that take place in the natural world. The photographer of the above optical illusion was lucky enough to snap this photo of a remarkable natural event. The setting sun looks like it is being cut in half by some passing clouds. What makes this optical illusion really amazing is the fact that the cloud cover gives the illusion that the sun is not only cut, but also disintegrating.

People who want to capture an optical illusion like this do not have to do too much but wait for the next cloudy day. The setting sun happens every night, which makes the chance of photographing an event such as this fairly high. The photographer should be standing on something high up in the air like a balcony or on a rooftop so that he or she is on the same level as the setting sun.

After so many years of owning a pet, a natural phenomenon takes place in which the pet owner begins to resemble their pet and vice versa. However, there are some times when people really can turn into their pet such as the above optical illusion. In this photograph, the woman has a dog for a head. The white fluffy dog also appears to be changing from a dog with white hair to a dog with brown hair.

In order to create this illusion, the woman held her dog up in such a way that blocks her own face. The person who took the photograph had to hold the camera up at eye level at the right moment when the picture was snapped. The owner of the dog also had to hold her pet up in such a way that covered her face completely, and then the picture was taken to create the optical illusion.

The above optical illusion is unique because it has a green dot in the middle. The green dot is in the center of a white background with gray stripes. If people were to stare at the green dot in the center, they will notice that something is happening to the gray stripes. The longer people stare at the center green dot, the more and more faded the gray stripes will look. If people continue to gaze at the green dot, eventually the stripes will disappear entirely.

When people stare at something for a long enough time, their eye muscles will start to relax. In order to create this illusion, all people need to do is create a white background, add some diagonal gray stripes, and then put a bright colored dot in the middle of it.

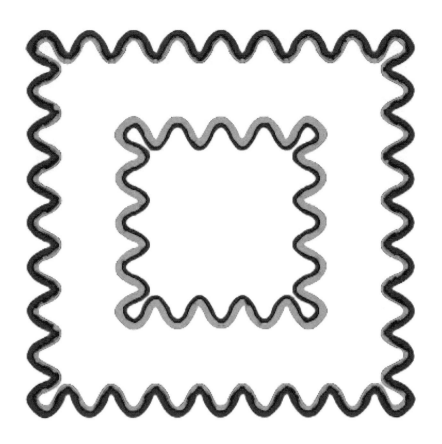

The above image is one larger square outlined in purple on the outside and orange on the inside. There is a second smaller square in the middle of the larger one that is the opposite, outlined in orange on the outside, but purple on the inside. Between the big square and the middle square is a light color. For those staring at these two squares, the section in the middle appears to be a light orange or beige color. However, the section between the big and small square is not light orange or beige, but it is actually white.

The center of the smaller square is actually white, but because of the fact that it is outlined in purple, the white can easily be seen. Because the large square is outlined in the orange color, and the inner circle has an outer orange outline, the section between the two squares appears to match the orange outlines.

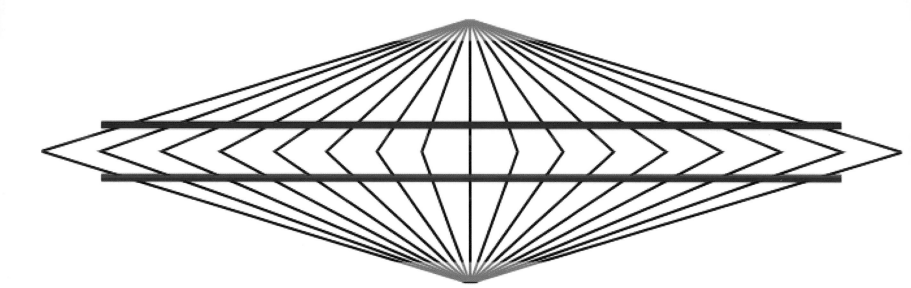

The above image is a white background that contains a diamond shape. The black lines begin at the top of the image and then begin to extend outwards. As the thin lines extend out, and then down, they bend in the middle, which gives the black diamond its shape. At the center of the black diamond, the lines all bend out, but there is a single straight line that remains at the top of the image and goes down to the bottom.

Across the center of the bending diamond are red lines and because the middle bends, it appears as though the red lines are bent as well. People who see the red lines are going to instantly think they are bent just like the middle of the diamond, but the fact is they are as straight as a ruler.

The above image is a simple white background that has black lines that go from one side of the image to the other. The lines start out small to match the corner of the square, then get bigger as they go across the image to the other corner where another small line has been placed. In order to make the lines look like they are bending, smaller lines have been added going from the top of the line to the bottom.

The position of the smaller line is what makes the long lines appear to be bent. Some of the smaller lines are placed at the same angle as the long line, but other smaller lines are pointing down. Because the smaller lines are on the white background, they force the eye to make the longer line look like it is bent in the same direction as the smaller lines applied to each one.

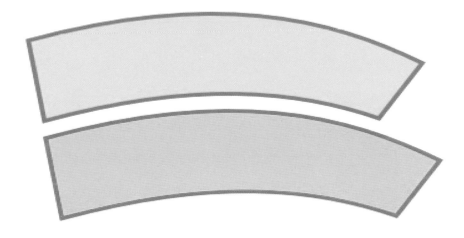

What people may not realize is that sometimes colors can create optical illusions all on their own. When people paint their homes, they may often choose a light color because it makes a room look bigger even if it really is not. In the above image, people are going to see a blue arch and a pink arch. At first glance, the two arches do not look like they are the same size; the pink one looks slightly bigger than the blue above it.

Out of the two colors, the pink color is lighter and it makes the arch look a lot longer than the blue. However, if people want to really find out what size the two arches are, they can always measure with a ruler to find out if the pink one is truly longer than the blue or if it just a trick of the eyes.

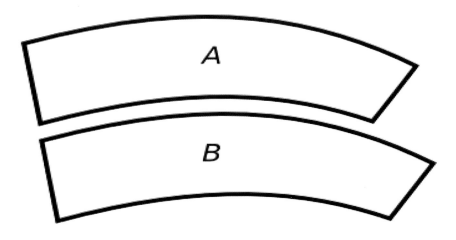

There is nothing simpler than two black and white arches. The image posted above has two arches that are labeled A and B. Arch A is on top of Arch B, but it looks like Arch B is a lot longer. However, if people were to actually measure the two arches, they will see that they are the exact same size. In the previous optical illusion, the fact that one arch is a different color than the other helped make one look bigger than the other, but these two arches are not colored at all.

What makes these two arches look like they are different sizes is the fact that they are stacked on top of one another and very close together. The eye is going to follow the slope of each arch, and Arch B looks longer because the arch on top of it gives something for it to be compared to.

A trip to the airport can be a lot of fun because it gives people the chance to see really big planes up close and personal without having to actually get on board one of them. While all planes may appear to be the same, this is not always the case, depending on what airplane manufacturer designed and built the plane. The above image is a picture of a plane, but it is also an optical illusion.

This plane does not look like a regular plane because it has certain features that make it look like there are two planes stacked on top of one another. The head of the plane has an extra bump on it, which can easily be mistaken for another plane. Also, the wings on this plane are high up on the top of it, which makes it look like a plane has pulled in right beside it.

There is nothing more fun than when winter comes and people can get out into the cool air and participate in some fun winter activities, such as sledding and ice skating. This optical illusion is all about skating under the light of the full moon. In order to see what they are doing, the skaters are carrying lanterns.

If people follow the ice skaters from the bottom of the image, and then go all the way to the top, it looks like the skaters, with their lanterns, are skating straight up into the sky and turning into the stars. Another way to look at this illusion would be that the stars came down from the sky to do a little night ice skating.

The most famous city in the world is arguably New York City. The Big Apple is known for many things, including its high rise buildings that stretch into the sky. The above image can be taken in more than one way. At first glance, people may say that the picture looks like a see-through glass building. However, there may be other people that see the dark shadow and think those are the buildings, but simply have a glass covering over them.

A third option for the above image can be that there are simply four glass buildings right next to one another, lined up as bowling pins with the dark shadows on them being a reflection of buildings that are across the street.

There are many talented artists in the world that are known for some of the world's most famous art, such as the Mona Lisa, which was painted by Leonardo da Vinci and is being displayed in Paris, France. However, not every work of art is painted on a piece of stretched canvas. These days, there are artists that use things like walls and buildings to display their works of art.

The above image is proof that even a building can be turned into a piece of art that people can actually live in. At first glance, people may see this triangle-shaped building and think that it is being renovated, but it is in fact painted to look like someone has sliced it up or is possibly renovating it.

When two weather fronts collide, the air can turn thick and damp, which is also known as fog. In some areas of the world, like London and San Francisco, the fog can be so thick and heavy that it can literally stop traffic both on land and on water. Lighthouses were created to help ships on the water make it to shore, but sometimes the fog can be thick and impenetrable even with the brightest light.

The above picture is a fine example of how bad fog can be. The image is actually an optical illusion because the fog is so bad that it is impossible to tell whether the person on the far right is standing on land or standing in water.

Going to a beach is a great way to spend warm days. With the smooth white sand, and the cool blue water, a kid can really have a great time building sand castles or even going swimming. Some people take their swimming very seriously, and grab their scuba gear and take to the water to see what they can find just under the surface.

The above image shows that some kids love to scuba dive, but this young man is scuba diving in the middle of the air. Anyone that sees a boy floating in midair may wonder how this picture was taken, and the answer may be more complicated than people realize. The boy might be suspended in midair with wires, but there are no wires under him nor a trampoline to help get him airborne.

There is nothing quite like going to another country to see the sights. Traveling can be very relaxing for some people because they get a chance to get away from the pressures and stress of their everyday lives. People often take plenty of pictures while they are traveling and try to take the most unique photos they can. The above image shows two young men in another country as subjects of a very special photograph that has them upside down over a body of water. It does look like the two young men are about to fall into the water that shows the reflection of a city along a river.

People often have their very good friends over for dinner. There is nothing more relaxing than people all getting together to sit down and enjoy a fine meal together. However, some people just do not make good dinner guests. In the above image, a young woman has lost her head over a meal. It is not very difficult to tell that the above image is an optical illusion, because the young woman appears to be alive even with her head cut off.

How this optical illusion is done is pretty simple, and the answer lies under the table. It may not be easy to tell, but the table the young woman has her head on is not your average table, because there is a mirror under it that is actually hiding the rest of her body from being seen.

For people wondering just how these two people can look like angels, the answer is simple. The man and woman are standing in front of a bright blue wall that has two pairs of wings painted on it. In order to turn two humans into angels, all the man and woman had to do was stand in just the right position to give them both wings.

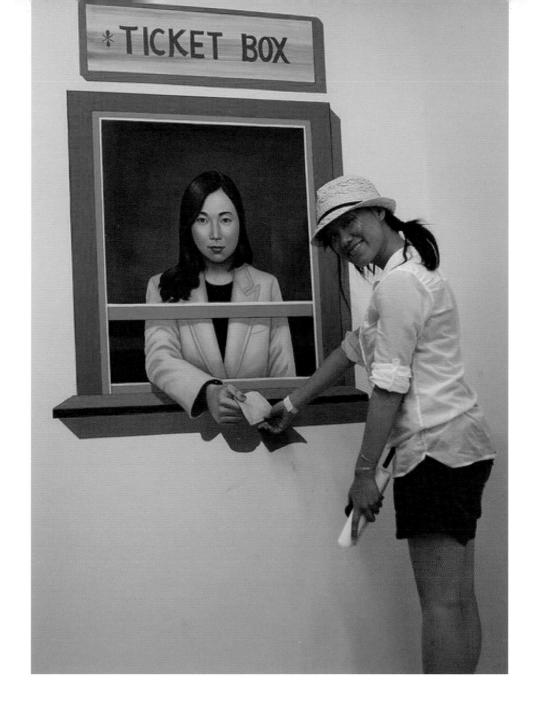

In the above image, a young woman is standing at a ticket booth buying a ticket, but stopped long enough to have her photograph taken. If people look closely at this photo, they will notice that the young woman is in fact buying a ticket from a painting on a wall. The image is painted so well, and looks so realistic, that people might not even be able to tell that the woman and the ticket booth are not real.

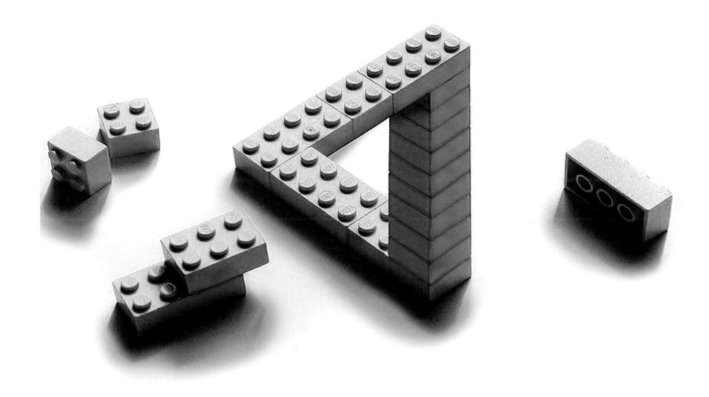

There are millions of kids around the world that love playing with blocks. With these blocks, kids are only limited by their imagination and can literally build anything they want. In the above image, these yellow blocks are stacked up in such a way that forms an optical illusion. The triangle is formed by yellow blocks, but the right side of it looks a little funny, because it appears to be standing up. However, people who are seeing this bright yellow triangle may notice that the triangle is not standing up, but is actually lying on its side. The clue that people need to look for is that the fact that one side of the triangle is not casting a shadow, which means that one side of the triangle is lying down and not standing up.

In the hole in the lawn, there is a picturesque scene with a few trees and an apartment building. If people are looking to relocate to a whole universe, all they have to do is fall into this hole and they may end up in someplace new and fascinating. There is an old saying that the grass is always greener on the other side, and this hole in the lawn just may prove it.

In the above image, two people are trying to disappear, and for the most part, they succeed all thanks to the background they are in front of and what they are carrying. The two people in the above image may need to practice a little more since their feet and legs can still be seen. How long did it take you to spot them?

There are bridges all over the world, but none like the one in the picture above. In the optical illusion, a bridge is going across the big ocean, but at the same time, it is transforming. When people look at the image above, they will see that the clouds are creating the ships. If people start from the end of the bridge, and go across to the sailing ship, they will see an amazing transformation from clouds to full-fledged sailing ship with masts, and flags on top waving in the breeze.

Forced Perspective

There is nothing more fun than traveling and taking pictures of the world's most famous landmarks. Italy is a very famous old country to travel to and explore. People want to go to this amazing old Mediterranean country to see things like the famous canals in Venice, but there are also other famous things to see like the Leaning Tower of Pisa. This optical illusion involves something called forced perspective, which was used in the famous *Lord of the Rings* and *The Hobbit* movies to make the hobbits really seem like very tiny people.

The way that forced perspective is done is a camera is placed at a very specific angle that makes anyone standing directly in front of the camera look very tall or very small. With this optical illusion, the tower and man actually look like the same size, and he is able to touch the Leaning Tower of Pisa.

Forced perspective can make average-sized people look like giants or it can make them look really small, which is a technique that is now being utilized in many blockbuster Hollywood films. All forced perspective does is force the eye to see people, who are standing a certain way or at a certain distance, appear to be a different size then they normally are.

This forced perspective picture involves making two camouflaged soldiers appear to be different sizes. The way this amazing illusion was done is that the person who looks really tiny is standing some distance away from his fellow soldier and the camera. The gigantic soldier is holding his hand out, and from this point of view, the soldier standing far away looks like he is standing in the palm of the gigantic soldier.

Anyone that has a child knows that they can grow rather fast, like weeds, but the above optical illusion shows that some kids can grow to be so tall they can outgrow their own home. This young man can stomp through a city, just like a famous movie monster. For those that are wondering just how this optical illusion is done, there are two ways that this might have been accomplished.

The young man might have taken the picture behind a green screen, which was then super imposed over a background of the buildings. Another way that this illusion could be created is the position of the camera. If a camera is placed on the ground pointed up, the young man would appear to be larger than his surroundings, especially if he is closer to the camera than the buildings.

Going out to the sand flats can be a lot of fun, especially if it gives two friends the chance to make a really neat optical illusion. The giant girl that lives on the sand flats has gotten herself a tiny captive, and then took a picture to immortalize her accomplishment. The way this illusion was done is rather simple. The photographer was with the young woman, but the third person in the picture, who played the tiny prisoner, was standing in the distance.

The timing of this picture has to be just right because the young woman has to have her hand up in just the right spot so it looks like the person in the distance is standing in the palm of her hand. Typically, an optical illusion like this might take more than one attempt in order for the palm of the hand, and the standing person, to line up just right.

The above photograph is an optical illusion that has a giant booted leg about to kick over a tall standing tower. People who see the above photograph may want to recreate it for themselves. In order to make a picture like the above illusion, all people need to do is pick a landmark that is in their area. The camera must be placed on the ground and tilted up at an angle that will show the whole landmark.

The person that will appear to kick the tower over has to estimate where to place their leg and then try it. From the low ground angle of the camera, the leg in the right position is going to appear to push the tower over. It may take many tries in order to get the angle of the camera and leg just right to create the optical illusion.

The above optical illusion shows a young man that is enjoying a quiet and peaceful day in the woods, but he happens to be sitting in the palm of someone else's hand. People who see this illusion may be wondering how the two people were able to pull off this amazing trick. The secret to this optical illusion is the angle of the photograph and the position that the young man is sitting.

The digital camera has to be set at a high angle, but pointed down so it is above the young man. The young man is actually sitting on a rock. In order to make it look like the young man is sitting in the hand of his friend, his friend has to be very close to the camera. The person standing near the camera has to stick their hand out and place it under the bottom of the sitting man in order to create this optical illusion.

People can take toys cars and have a whole lot of fun with them, like using them to create really neat optical illusions. What makes this optical illusion really unique is the fact that the photographer took this picture from a car window. The distance from the car to the parked car is just far enough to make the real car look a lot smaller than it actually is. The space between the photographer and the parked car is far enough to allow for the small red toy car to be placed in the empty parking space.

In order to create this optical illusion, the photographer may need to practice placing the toy car in the space in order to have the car line up just right with the parked car. The toy car also is very close to the curb and placed correctly between the white painted parking lines.

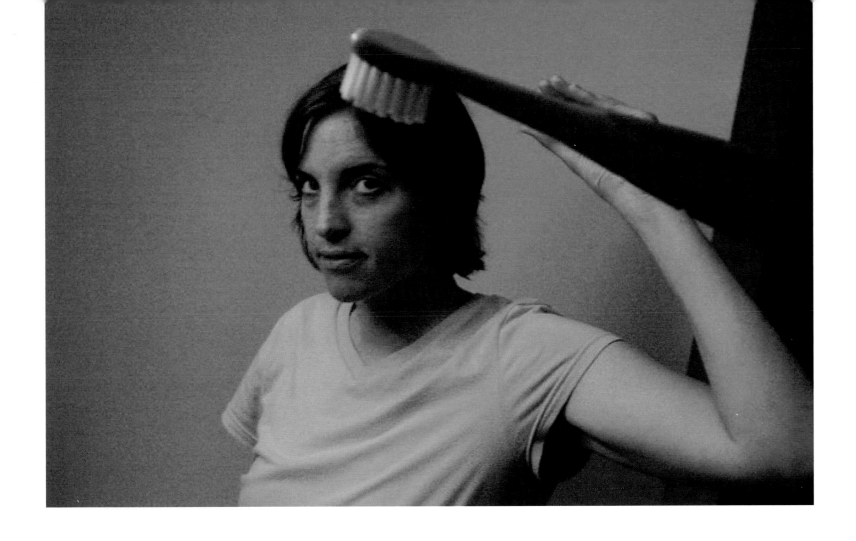

The world is full of people of different sizes. Though no matter what size people are, they have to do things like take showers, brush their teeth, and brush their hair. The above optical illusion shows a woman that appears to be pretty small. The woman is so small that is looks like she can brush her hair with a toothbrush. In order to do this optical illusion, the woman and the photographer have to be standing a few feet apart. The farther away the photographer stands, the smaller the woman is going to look.

When the woman and the photographer are the right distance apart, the normal-sized toothbrush is going to look a lot bigger than it really is. The woman has to hold her arm up at just the right angle in order to look like she is holding the handle of the toothbrush. After a few practice shots, the woman can put her arm up and create a really neat optical illusion.

There are many structures around the world that are architectural wonders. Some of these structures are so enormous that it is often believed that they were created by other means than the hands of man, such as the Great Pyramids of Giza located in Egypt. However, the picture to the left just may lend some validity to all of the theories that those Giza pyramids, and other super structures, were indeed created by supernatural forces.

This amazing structure appears to have been created by two gigantic hands, and someone was lucky enough to get a photograph of them. Though this picture appears to be genuine, the truth is that it was created using a regular digital camera placed at just the right angle, with someone simply raising their hands as if holding the structure up.

There are people out there that make it their mission in life to take the most unusual photographs possible. This person was out in the salt flats, with a bottle of water, and decided to turn it into a very unique image. There are a couple of ways that this picture could have been taken. The first way is taking a picture of the bottle, and then the person standing on top of it was actually superimposed into the image.

The second way that this image could be created was that the person on top was added in later with the help of a software program such as Photoshop. Because the image is so sharp and clear, the real answer to how this image was taken could be that it is in fact two combined pictures.

In the above image, a giant child has taken a woman captive. The way that this neat photograph could have been taken is the person with the camera took a picture first of the child pointing down, and then a second picture was taken with the woman standing in just the right place to make it look like she is being held down by the child's finger.

Some people really love balconies, because they can step out onto them and observe a spectacular view. In order for those balconies to be safe, there are railings around them preventing people from falling a great distance down to the ground. Every once in a while, the balcony railing is going to need some repair work, and it takes several volunteers to pull off this task.

The above picture looks like a group of people repairing the balcony railing. However, what people may not realize is that the above image is not really balcony repair, but is actually an optical illusion. The people in this picture are actually helping to pull the illusion off thanks to their use of the ropes and standing in just the right place.

In the above image, a tiny man is standing next to a gigantic rabbit. Anyone that sees this image is probably wondering just how is it that the rabbit could get so big that it could literally bend down and eat the small man. Since rabbits really do not grow to be this big, clearly this picture was done with forced perspective that makes the rabbit appear to be gigantic in comparison to the man.

Going out to see the tourist attractions that a place has to offer can be very tiring. After so many museums, people are bound to get hungry, but the last place that people expect to find a meal is at a place that people go for an education. However, in the above image, a young woman is getting a big piece of sushi to snack on. What makes this image really interesting is the fact that the young woman is not eating at a café or restaurant, but instead one of the paintings she is looking at is actually feeding her the sushi.

Artistic Optical Illusions

3D Pac-Man

Are you lucky enough to remember the Pac-Man game originally introduced in the early 1980s? Even if you never played the game before, you're likely familiar with the characters and the concept, as Pac-Man is known for being one of the most popular video games of all time, as well as an icon of early '80s pop culture.

The game must have had a lasting effect on artist Leon Keer, as he dedicated a whole piece of street art to Pac-Man.

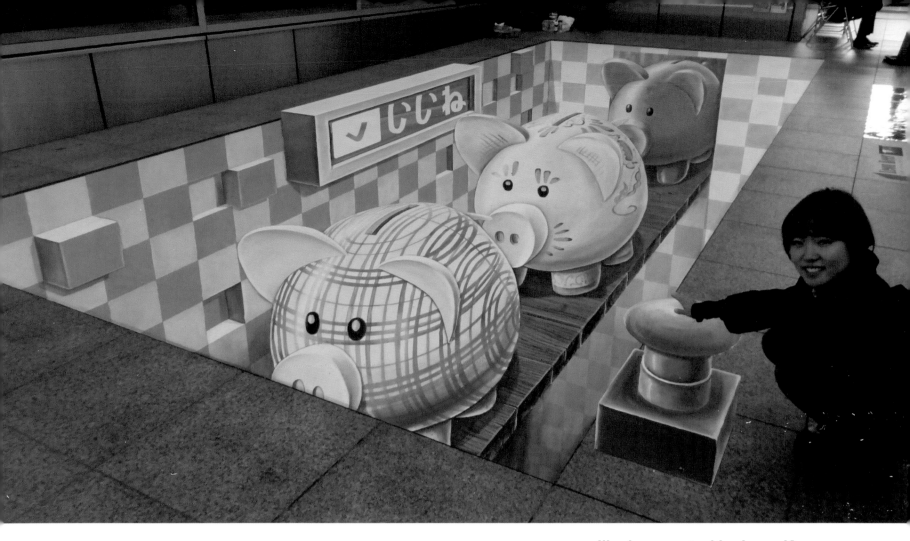

3D Piggy Bank

The illusion above, which was displayed in Fukuoka, Japan, goes by the title *Piggy Bank*. As you can see in the above 3D chalk drawing, there are numerous piggy banks placed on something like a factory line. There's also a start/stop control button, which the young lady in the picture appears to be pressing. This is yet another amazing illusion by the talented Leon Keer, who enables his viewers to interact with his amazing pieces of art.

3D Space Invaders

It looks like Leon Keer enjoys video games, as he presents to us another video game–inspired piece of street art. In this image, you can see a 3D rendition of the popular video game Space Invaders. Space Invaders was extremely successful at the time of its release and is known for being one of the major reasons video gaming is so popular today. It helped take video games from being a little corner-market niche and expanded them into the global sensation that they are today.

3D Claw Machine

The 3D chalk image above was put on display at the Sarasota Chalk Festival. As you can see in the image, the design was inspired by a claw machine game that you'll find in any arcade. However, the one in the image seems to combine both futuristic and antique concepts to give off the unique design that you see above. This illusion would also allow viewers to interact with it if given the right angle. Just imagine someone standing in front of the machine and appearing to have a finger on the red button, while their hand seemingly wrapped around the joystick.

Cons Space

The image you see above was on display at Cons Space Berlin, which is a festival that celebrates art, music, and skating. In the image above, it looks as if a girl has climbed to the top of a building and she's spray painting graffiti on the side of it. Also, Leon Keer used real-life props, such as the paint can on the right side of the chalk drawing, to interact with the art, which adds to the effect.

Glass House Theatre

The above drawing is known as the Glass House Theatre and was on display in Rosny-sous-Bois, France. As you can see, it looks as if a girl is trapped inside of a glass enclosure. On her left side is a real-life woman interacting with the piece of art, which makes the effect that much more intense.

Illusion created by Leon Keer

Iron Jacks

Everyone loves a good bowl of cereal, except for the guy in the image above, as he seems to be kicking a whole box of Iron Jacks over with a grin on his face. This is another beautiful piece of artwork drawn by the hands of master artist Leon Keer, and was put on display in Sarasota, Florida. What's amazing about this piece is that it's drawn in a way that allows his audience to interact with the piece of art, which truly brings it to life.

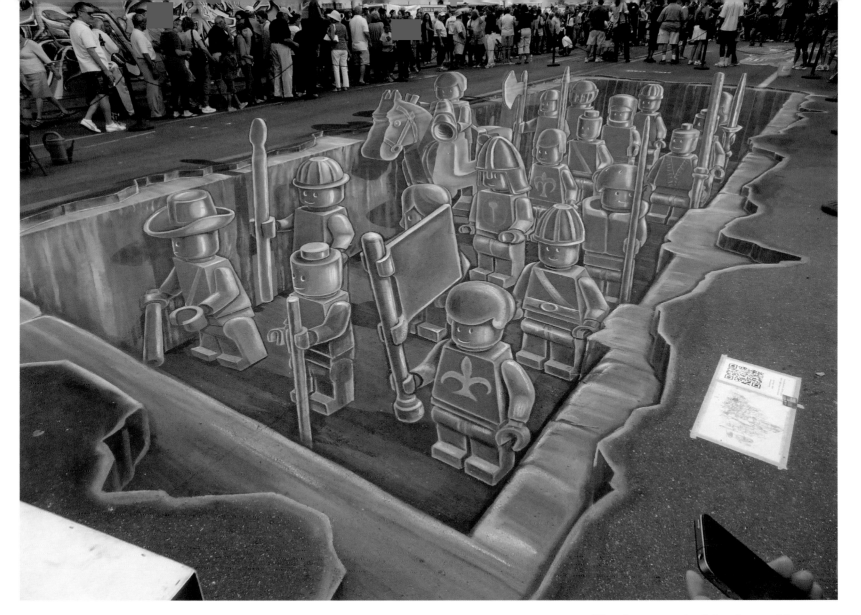

Illusion created by Leon Keer

Lego Terracotta Army

Leon Keer presented this piece of artwork once again at the Chalk Festival in Sarasota, Florida, which shows off an army made up of Lego characters. However, instead of it looking as if they're marching down the street, it looks as if they're marching underneath the pavement, through the dirt, which gives the illusion a nice, vintage effect.

Illusion created by Leon Keer

Side Effect

The image above goes by the title *Side Effect* and, like a lot of Leon Keer's work, it was on display at the Chalk Festival in Sarasota, Florida. As you can see, it looks like a Lego figure may be in a bit of trouble and is in need of resuscitation. It looks like the woman in the image may be trying to help the little guy out, as she could be giving him a shot of some adrenaline. Either way, it's a cool effect and the use of a model really brings the whole image to life.

Illusion created by Leon Keer

Time to Play

The above drawing goes by the title of *Time to Play* and was on display in Wijnegem, Belgium. In the image, we see a man sitting on a spring-loaded seat that's inside of a car. Due to the interaction of a real-life model, it gives the drawing a much more realistic effect, which Leon Keer is known for. Most of his pieces of art allow people to interact with them, which adds greatly to the overall effect.

Victim of Circumstance

The above artwork goes by the title of *Victim of Circumstance* and was on display in Bangkok, Thailand. As you can see, a child has been connected to a video game controller, which may lead you to believe that you would be able to completely control a child with nothing more than a few buttons and a joystick. It's very interesting to think about the message that Leon Keer may be trying to get across with this work of art.

Illusion created by Leon Keer

Virtual Transition of Raw Art

The above image, titled *Virtual Transition of Raw Art*, was put on display in Rotterdam, Netherlands. Once again, Leon Keer has created a piece of art that enables viewers to interact with it, which makes the piece that much more fascinating, as it adds a sense of realism to his work.

Illusion Created By: T.A.L.E.N.T. Murals Inc.

Pungo Off Road Shop

This is yet again another garage door that has been meticulously painted by the hands of Todd and Eric Lindbergh of T.A.L.E.N.T. Murals Inc. to look like an active garage. As you can see, there's a real vehicle parked in front of the garage to add to the realistic effect these two were trying to achieve. Chances are, if you passed this mural on the road, you probably wouldn't even think twice about stopping in at this garage for your annual tune-up.

Garage Work

If you drove by this scene on the street, you probably wouldn't even take a second look at it. After all, it's likely an image you see fairly often while you're driving through your neighborhood. There's nothing spectacular or peculiar about this scene. It looks like nothing more than someone doing a bit of maintenance work on their classic car while their garage door is open.

However, there *is* something special about this scene, because you're staring at nothing more than a mural painted on a closed garage door.

Illusion created by T.A.L.E.N.T. Murals Inc.

Hot Rod Van

T.A.L.E.N.T. Murals Inc. specializes in creating piece of art that will definitely make the viewer take a second look. As a matter of fact, the art is so well done that most people don't even know they're staring at a work of art. For instance, in this picture, it looks like a van is parked beside an old school hot rod, but don't let it fool you. The hot rod was actually painted on the side of the van by T.A.L.E.N.T. Murals Inc.

There was a video game back in the 1980s called Q-Bert. The video game was very popular because of its simple concept and design. The object of the game was to guide a small orange animal down a huge stack of 3D blocks that looked kind of like stairs while avoiding a small ball that was also bouncing down the steps.

When people played the game long enough, the squares that were both light and dark seemed to come right off of the screen. The above image looks just like that old Q-Bert game. The contrast between the light gray and dark gray squares come together to form blocks. If people stare at this image long enough, the squares do take on a 3D appearance.

Chess and checkers are two of the most popular board games that people play. The board is covered in black and white checkers that people place the game pieces on. Because the game board is both black and white, sometimes the two contrasting colors can actually play tricks on people's eyes. The above image is a black and white checkerboard, but there is something in the middle of that board that is going to make the human eyes dance around a bit.

The squares in the center are misshapen. When people stare at those distorted squares long enough they are in for a surprise. There is a hidden circle that can only be seen when people gaze at the misshapen blocks. After a minute or two of an uninterrupted gaze, the center circle will become a 3D image that will come to life.

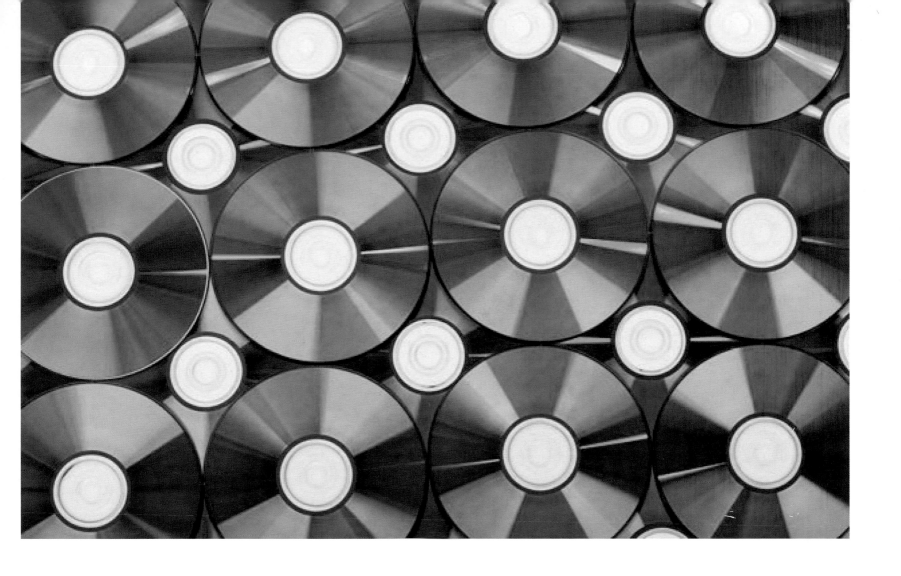

Compact discs first came into the world during the mid 1980s. Also known as CDs, these remarkable shiny discs replaced the square plastic tapes. People were skeptical about CDs at first, but the sound quality was a lot better than the thin cellophane-like material that was inside each cassette tape. The back of each CD is remarkable because it gives off a rainbow when light is shined on it.

The above image is a bunch of compact discs all put together. The discs usually have holes in the center of them, but for this image, the center of them is white. In order to see the compact discs spin, people just need to stare at the bright white center. As people look at the CD's middle, the light will catch the shiny outer edge and begin to spin.

A red background can be very eye-catching, especially when it is combined with black, white, and gray. The image is a gray circle, but the center of it is a checkerboard design. In order to see the optical illusion, people have to stare at the black and white checkers in the center of the circle. As people stare at the middle, they will see the black and white squares form a circle.

However, the center circle is not the only image that can be seen. The outer edge of the circle is another optical illusion that also starts to slowly spin the longer people stare at it. To add to the fun of the circles, the very outer edge of the gray circle is going to move slightly because the black and white squares are put so close together.

Black and white checkers combine together to make a really neat background. The above image is a black and white checkered background, but there is something very special located in it. A hint for people who do not see the something special right away should stare directly at the center and see what image appears.

The circle is formed because the black and white checkers around the edge of it are a different size then the ones on the outside and on the inside. A simple distortion of the squares can make all the difference, especially when it comes to the making of optical illusions. Also, as people stare at the globe, they may notice that it appears to be moving out toward the viewer.

The above image bears a striking resemblance to the human eye, with a large outer circle that looks like an eyeball and a smaller inner circle that looks like the pupil. If people look at the pupil, they may notice that its gray blurry center appears to be pulsing. In order to make this large eye appear to be expanding and contracting, the creator of this illusion used the two opposing colors of black and white.

To create the eye itself, there are white angled stripes along the outer edge. The black and white checkers along the pupil allow the image to pulsate and go from large to small, much like when the pupil within the eye focuses whenever light hits it or when there is very little light.

Anyone that wants to create their very own optical illusion needs to have a couple of things in order to make it work. A background of two contrasting colors, such as black and white, has to be used. The black and white should be patterned and checkers is the easiest pattern to create. The next thing needed for the illusion is a shape of some kind that will appear to move in some way.

For the above illusion, a pentagon is placed in the center of the black and white checkered background. To create the pulsating pentagon, each section of the shape has checkers that are facing opposite directions. When looking at the center pentagon, the surrounding checkered pattern will give the illusion that the pentagon is thumping out and back in.

When the breeze is blowing nice and strong, every flag in the world waves in such a nice way that people cannot help but stop and watch. Many people enjoy watching the flags blowing in the breeze and consider it to be quite soothing. However, whenever people see a flag fluttering in the wind, they often want to recreate it in their own homes on their personal computers. Creating a waving flag is not hard as long as it is done in just the right way.

Black and white checkers can be used in a specific way to simulate the effect of waving. The checkers have to be placed on the background in different ways that have the checkers going on their left side, then flat, and then going on the right side. The eye will follow the squares as they go from one side to another, which will make the whole image look like it's rolling along just like a flag waving in the breeze.

Sometimes when patterns are put together, they inadvertently cause an optical illusion. The above image is a gray background with black and white diamonds and thick gray lines that move from the center of the image outward. However, the first thing that anyone is going to notice is the crocodile-like teeth that are slowly going around and around the image. While the crocodile teeth are clearly seen, the fact is that they were not purposely added to the background.

If people look closely, they will see that the teeth are created from the combination of the gray lines and the black and white diamonds. The white color is not very easy to see among the diamond shapes, but it is there helping to make the crocodile teeth look like they are standing out.

Any shape or image that is put against a black and white checkered background is going to immediately stand out just because the two colors are opposite of one another. In order to make a 3D illusion, people need to use a background of two colors in which one is light and one is dark. Since there are so many colors to choose from, people typically just go with black and white because they are very easy to work with.

The above image is a fine example of a 3D image that shows a swirl that contains black and white checkers. Moving from the outside toward the center, the squares are getting smaller with each level, which makes the swirl stand out and become three dimensional.

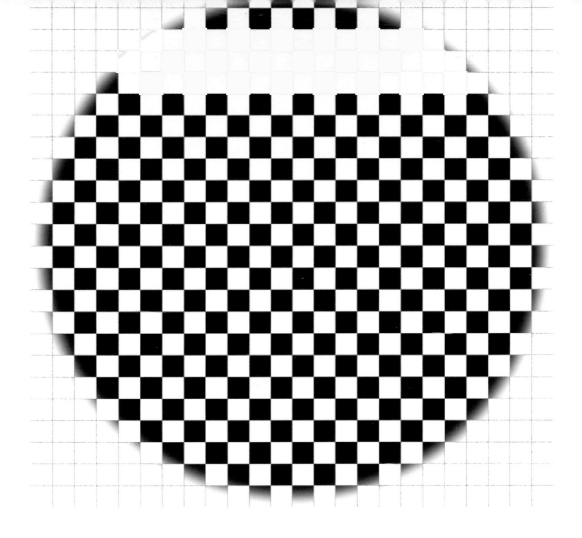

There are some colors that can overtake others. White and black are the two most common colors and they can work together beautifully to create anything from works of art to optical illusions. In the above image, the background is pure white, but it looks like a piece of graph paper that is often used for math problems such as geometry. What makes graph paper special is the fact that the lines can help create graphs, which is an essential part of certain kinds of math.

The center of the graph paper contains a circle that is filled with white and black checkers. The outline of the circle has half of the black squares turning white. However, because the graph paper is white, and combined with the half black and half white squares, the white looks like it is spreading and covering the checkered squares.

When there are white and black checkers involved in an image, there are many things that can happen if the checkers are used in just the right way. It is always a lot fun to experiment with the two colors of black and white to see what happens. The above image is a fine example of the fading effect. The squares start on the right side of the image, and then go across to the other side. However, on the right side, the black and white checkers are clearly seen, but as they go across the image, their size begins to shrink. By the time the eye has gone to the left side of the image, the black and white squares are so tiny that it looks like the whole wall is just slowly fading away.

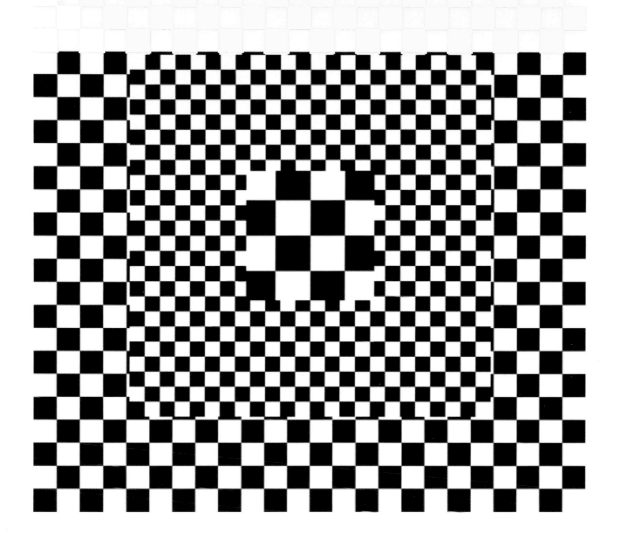

The country of Egypt has ancient pyramids that attract millions of people globally to see the most impressive structures in the world. It is still a mystery how these amazing pyramids were created, but they are so well built they will probably last for thousands of years more. Some people will never get to travel to Egypt, but that does not mean that they can deny themselves the fun and excitement of seeing a pyramid with their very own eyes.

The image above is a black and white checkered background that has a center square with smaller square, and a third square of very large checkers. When people stare at the large center square, the section with the smaller squares is going to stand out and create a pyramid that can be seen from the top down.

The image above has more than one option when it comes to the optical illusion that can be seen. The background of black and white squares is what is often used to create an optical illusion. To really make an image stand out, what is placed on top of the checkers background are smaller triangles with gray and white square that go in different directions. When people look at this image, they can see small pyramids or they might see something else.

The pyramids also form a second illusion that looks just like stars. The more people stare at the center of the image, the clearer the illusions will become. Whether people see the pyramids or the stars, the above image is certainly interesting enough to keep people trying to figure out which images they see.

Anyone that has ever stared at a chain link fence for too long may experience an optical illusion. Sometimes when staring at the criss-cross shapes that are created by the fencing, the triangles created can come right out toward people just like any other 3D image. The above image is a recreation of a chain link effect. The checkered background has another image on top of it that helps create the 3D effect.

When staring long enough at the lighter gray triangles that are placed over the background, the glass-like look of the image starts to stand out. If people gaze long enough at the glass-like triangles, they are going to see them start to move. Also, the longer people watch the image, the blurrier the black and white squares get, which can make the image hard to look at after a while.

The above image is of a black and white checkered ball, but there is something not quite right about it. If people start at the top of this black and white ball, and then work their way down, they are going to see that there are cracks in the ball. If people look at the cracks closely, the cracks are not only spreading from the top to the bottom, but they are also sinking into the ball as well.

To help make the image complete, there are patches of bright white light that are on the ball. The white patches really help the cracks stand out. What also helps people see the spreading cracks is the fact that the black and white checkered ball is on a solid light-colored background.

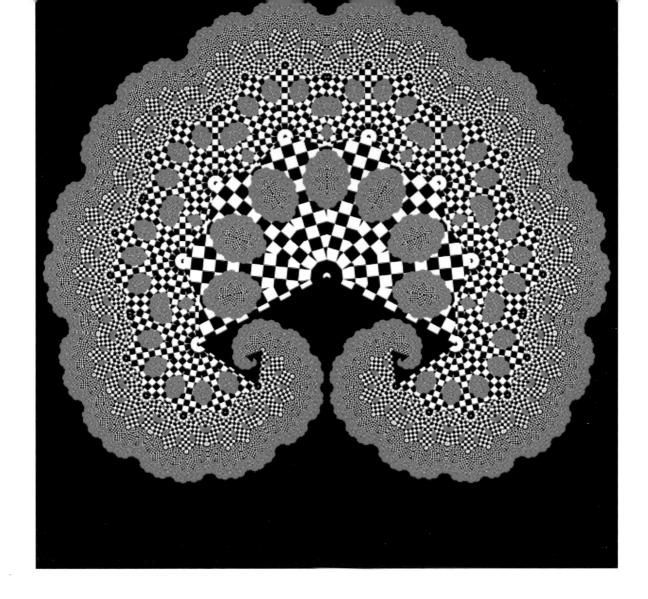

There are literally thousands of ways that a checkerboard image can be used, but the above image is one of the most unique. The background of this checkerboard image is black, which means that the eyes are immediately drawn to whatever is in the center of that dark background. Inside the checkered image is black and white checkers, but they are used in unique designs that really give the impression that the center is moving.

What also helps the center images move is the fact that the outer edge of the image also has black and white checkers. For anyone that stares at the center long enough, they may say that the center of this round image looks very much like a crystal geode.

This black and white checkered background is of a simple design, but it also contains four gray-lined squares located in the very center. At first glance, there seems to be nothing remarkable about the above image, but this is an incorrect assumption. The longer that people stare at those four squares, or at least one square, they are going to start to notice a couple of things.

The gray squares are going to start to pulsate. However, the center of the squares is the black and white squares, but they too are going to start to change. As people lock their gazes on those four squares, they will see that the inside part of the squares is going to start to get blurry and difficult to look at for any long period of time.

This above black and white background contains a starburst in the very center of it. If people really give the image the once over, they will notice that the starburst is actually taking the color out of the black and white checkers. Because the very center of the black and white background is unaffected, that small area looks a lot brighter than the rest of the image. The longer that people stare at the starburst, the more faded the black and white background appears to get. The lines protruding out from the center of the starburst are going across the whole background, and anything they touch seems to be slightly blurry. People are going to see that the starburst is turning many of the checkered squares gray, which is slowly taking the color out of the background as a whole.

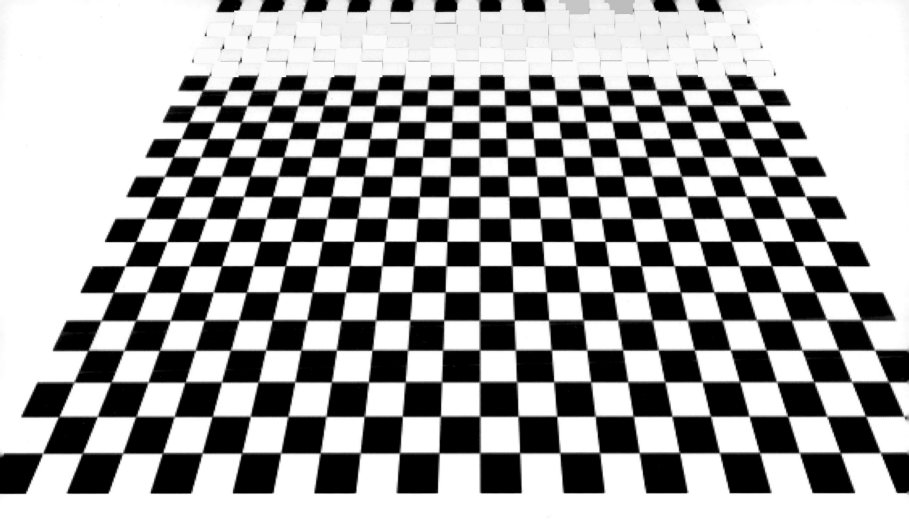

The world can be a different place depending on the point of view of the people that are in it. The above image is a checkered background, but the perspective of it is vertical. What makes this image special is the fact that the squares from the top to the bottom seem to be getting bigger, but that is actually not the case. Whether people believe it or not, the squares at the top of the image are the exact same size as the squares that are located at the very bottom. People who want to see another part of this optical illusion just need to stare at the squares along the bottom. After a few seconds of staring, the whole background looks as if the top of it is starting to rise up like one half of a seesaw.

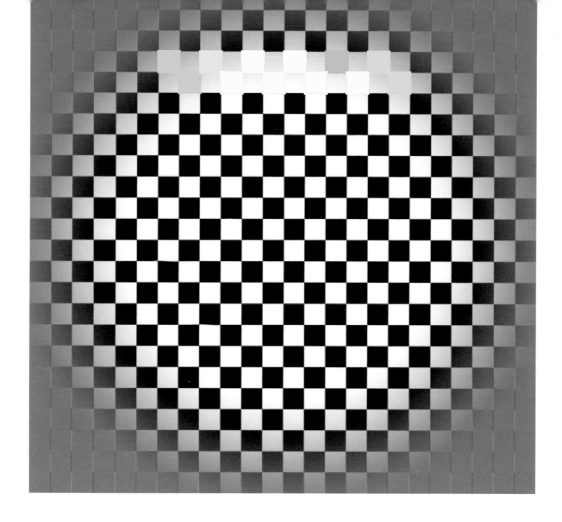

Anyone that has seen a horror movie, or has taken a trip to San Francisco, will understand just how thick fog can get. The above image is a checkered background that has fog around the very outer edge. Because the outside of the image is a light gray, the inner part of the image seems very bright. If people want to see something interesting, all they need to do is stare at that bright black and white center.

The more people stare at the black and white, the more the gray on the outside seems to be moving in just like the fog on a cold day. To complete the illusion, the squares on the outside area are also turning gray, which only helps the foggy areas look like they are spreading over the checkered background.

This optical illusion is one that can definitely make the eyes go crazy. The above image is a typical black and white squared checkerboard, but there is something else over it that actually turns it into a pretty neat optical illusion. There is what looks like a wire mesh over the checkers. When people gaze at the wire mesh long enough, there are a couple of things that can happen. Some people may stare at the image, and see the extra wire mesh covering disappear.

The second thing that may happen is that when people stare at the image, the wire mesh covering may actually start to separate from the checkerboard image. Whether the mesh disappears, or separates from the background, the illusion is pretty interesting.

The eye is naturally drawn to the large swirls because they are bigger than anything else. The longer people stare at the big swirls, the more it looks like those swirls are suspended in the air above the background.

There are a lot of talented artists in this world that prefer to use the human body instead of a typical canvas. The above image features a human model that has been painted to look like a speeding cheetah. In order to help the model not be seen, the image was created in a white room. To help the young woman blend in to the background, the model has also been painted white, including her hair.

It is quite amazing how much detail can be accomplished using a human model versus a canvas. The features of the cheetah can be easily seen, down to every spot on its muscular body. The artist did a fine job of showing just how majestic these big cats look when they run—even on a human canvas.

Anyone that has ever painted a house knows that the combination of light and dark colors is what is best to make a room look bigger or smaller. The above image is a fine example of painted walls, but it is also an optical illusion. If people see three painted walls, they may think that they are looking at the corner of the room. However, another way of looking at this image is seeing the edge of something like the side of a cabinet or a dresser.

How this illusion was created is simple, because of the left wall that is painted dark. If people follow along the top of the wall, their eyes will go right into the corner, but if people follow along the bottom of the wall they will see the edge of the cabinet or dresser.

At least once a year, people leave their homes to go someplace else for a little rest and relaxation with those that mean the most to them. While out of town, people might stay in a resort that often has a lot of great amenities and activities, such as going for a swim, exercising, gambling, and other sources of fun. However, for people who are not able to escape their hometown for someplace else, there are always other ways to relax and have a good time.

The above optical illusion shows three people that are enjoying a water slide. If people look closely, they will notice that the slide is not a real slide, but a rather intricate 3D chalk drawing on concrete that looks so real people can actually use it.

There are some places around the world that have the most remarkable kind of architecture that brings millions of tourists all around the world to see it. Some major cities try and take those most famous architecture buildings, and try to copy it so that it too will bring tourists, but not every city can afford to redo dozens of buildings in their downtown area. One way to cut the corners on spending millions of dollars on giving every older building a facelift is to simply recreate those remarkable buildings with a mural.

The above illusion shows that a paint job can be so good that it can fool anyone that looks at it into thinking the building has a fancy design when it really does not. A talented artist can paint a mural on a building and make it look like a totally different one with just a little paint and a lot of imagination.

Back in the 1940s and 1950s, there were a lot of cartoons that made the joke that if people dug a deep enough hole, they would end up digging straight to China. While everyone knows that digging a hole does not lead one to China, the joke was funny while it lasted. The above image brings people back to the olden days when that joke was still around.

There are two people that look like they are about to fall into a hole that leads them right to a Chinese temple. However, if people look close enough, they will see that the two people are walking, not falling, and the hole that is under their feet is actually a pretty realistic-looking 3D chalk drawing created by a talented artist.

Men and women often exercise in order to keep their bodies in top physical condition. After exercising for so long, people will end up with a lot of strong muscles that make exercising a bit easier for them. In the above image, a young man is sitting in a chair showing off just how strong he is. With his one index finger, the young man is able to lift a very heavy barbell without any strain at all. However, if people look closely, they will see that the young man is not as strong as he appears to be.

The above image is really a painting on a wall that the young man is sitting under. In order to appear to be super strong, all the young man has done is put his hand under the barbell with his index finger extended up like he is lifting the weight.

This delivery truck contains what looks like boxes of equipment. However, there is a problem with the above delivery truck, because it looks like the truck driver has forgotten to close the back door of his truck. If the driver happens to hit a bump, he is in danger of losing all of his cargo. People may be trying to tell the driver that the backdoor is open, but the driver knows a secret about the back of his truck. The reality of the situation is that the back of the truck is not actually open, but is in fact painted to look like it is.

A long time ago, carnivals featured more than just games and the occasional circus act. Some carnivals featured a high diving act where a young man would climb up a very high ladder, and then jump into a big metal pool full of water. After some time, the high diving act eventually stopped taking place, but it was replaced with a lot of other great acts that people paid a lot of money to see.

In the above image, the high dive act has returned, but there is a little surprise for whoever decides to dive off of the diving board. If people look closely, they will see that a very large alligator is in the pool, which will make for quite an exciting time if someone were brave enough to jump into the pool.

Some places in the world are quite hazardous, because they are filled with dangerous animals like piranhas, lions, tigers, and crocodiles. While these dangerous locations are all over the world, it would be very unlikely for people to run into man-eating lions or crocodiles in your average city. However, with the above optical illusion, anything can happen, including dangerous man-eating animals showing up in the most unlikely places.

In the above image, a giant pit filled with green water, and dangerous crocodiles, has appeared in a city. People are not sure what to make of it and one man is so close to a crocodile that he might end up losing his head.

The great thing about an optical illusion is the fact that a talented artist can really make anything look like something else, no matter what it is. The above image is an alligator, but it is not one that is found in any swamp in the world. It may be hard to tell that this is not a real alligator because the artist has done such a good job of including the finest details that real alligators have.

The alligator is actually a hand with the thumb tucked in to simulate the lower jaw. Also, the artist has painted an eye at the top of the index finger knuckle, and every single scale is painted on the hand. It must have taken the artist a long time to turn this human hand into an alligator, but it looks so amazing the time was well worth it.

Animated Optical Illusions

Illusion created by Mark Grenier

Antithesis

Does the optical illusion in the picture above seem to be moving on its own, despite the fact that it's a static image? Stare at the black dot in the center of the image and you'll see what I'm talking about, if you haven't done so already. First of all, you're probably impressed at how amazing this illusion looks in general, but you're also probably wondering how illusions like the one above work.

The illusion above relies on your eyes to create the illusion that the image is moving or "dancing," as some prefer to call it. Fast eye movements, also known as saccades, as well as blinking, give off the illusionary effect. In other words, it's just your eyes playing tricks on you.

Illusion created by Mark Grenier

Collide-O-Scope

The above image, which goes by the title *Collide-O-Scope*, was created by Mark Grenier, who specializes in animated illusions. If you stare into the center of this image, you'll encounter an effect that makes it seem as if the lines in the image are pulsating. Go ahead, concentrate on the center of the image for a couple seconds and you'll begin to see the lines pulsating or "dancing," as some people like to say. Illusions like this are created by rapid eye movements, also known as saccades, and blinking.

Illusion created by Mark Grenier

Dazzle Wheels

The image you see above goes by the title of *Dazzle Wheels*, which is certainly a suitable name. Despite the fact that the image is static, it still seems to be moving on its own. Stare at the center of the image, in the blue area, and you'll begin to notice that all of the wheels in the image begin to turn on their own, sort of like the inner workings of a clock.

Illusion created by Mark Grenier

Eccentric Wheels

The above illusion goes by the title of *Eccentric Wheels*, which totally fits the illusion itself. If you stare at the center of the image, in the white space right in the middle, you'll encounter a mind-blowing effect. It seems as if the wheels in the image are moving on their own, despite the fact that it's a static image. Illusions like this basically work off of your eyes, using rapid eye movements, also known as saccades, and blinking to power the illusion.

Illusion created by Mark Grenier

Floating Spheres

The above illusion goes by the title of *Floating Spheres*. Just by staring at the illusion for a very brief period of time, you'll likely notice the illusion almost immediately. If not, you should stare at the center of the image and the illusion should come to life shortly thereafter. Despite being a static image, it looks as if the spheres are rotating in opposite directions. Your own eyes are responsible for creating the illusion that you see above. Rapid eye movements, known as saccades, and blinking give off the effect that the static image is actually animated.

Illusion created by Mark Grenier

Here's Looking At U

The title of the illusion you see above is *Here's Looking at U*. Once again, this is another illusion that seems to be animated, even though it's obviously a static image. If you don't see the effect immediately, just stare at the circle in the center of the image and you'll soon notice that the larger circles surrounding it begin to rotate in clockwise and counter clockwise fashion. Illusions like this are given power by your own eyes. With a combination of rapid eye movements and blinking, you're able to see the illusion above.

I Get Around

The illusion above goes by the title *I Get Around.* Mark Grenier is an illusionist that specializes in creating static images that have an animated effect to them. Without a doubt, this is one of his most stunning creations, as there's tons of movement going on in the image above. Chances are, you were able to see the illusionary effect almost immediately. If you didn't see the effect, try staring at the center of the image for a couple seconds, and you'll soon start to see the circles in the image beginning to move on their own.

Illusion-O

This illusion goes by the title of *Illusion-O.* This illusion is very similar to another illusion in Mark Grenier's lineup, which was titled *I Get Around.* It's nearly the same illusion, but with just a few slight modifications, including inverted colors. However, it's still an amazing illusion that gives off a beautiful animated effect when you look at it.

Illusion created by Mark Grenier

Jaggy Wheels Design

The above illusion goes by the title of *Jaggy Wheels Design*. This illusion definitely jumps right off the page at you, primarily due to the fact that it's in hot pink, but it's also an animated illusion, despite being a static image. In order to see the effect, you should just stare at the center of the illusion for a couple seconds and then you'll be able to see the wheels in the illusion beginning to spin. Illusions like this are powered by your own eyes. They play off of rapid eye movements, also known as saccades, as well as blinking in order to achieve the given effect.

Illusion created by Mark Grenier

Kinda Busy

The illusion you see in the image above is titled *Kinda Busy*. The image is completely static, yet there's an animated effect. If you don't see the effect, carefully scan the image with your eyes, going all over it, for a few seconds, and then you'll surely be able to see the desired effect. Suddenly, you noticed that the image begins to pulsate or "dance," as some people like to say. These illusions rely on your eyes to give off the desired effect. Basically, with rapid eye movements, also known as saccades, and blinking, you'll encounter the effect you see in the image above.

Mystic Spin Balls

The above illusion was given the title *Mystic Spin Balls*, by its creator, Mark Grenier. In this illusion, you'll encounter three balls that somewhat resemble bloodshot eyeballs. If you scan over the three balls with your eyes, you'll begin to notice that the image gives off an amazing 3D illusion. The balls in the image will look as if they're rotating in both a clockwise and counter clockwise fashion. Illusions like this rely on your eyes to achieve the effect that you see in the image. Basically, rapid eye movements, known as saccades, and blinking will give off the effect that the static image is actually animated.

Nine-Moon Marvel

The illusion you seen in the image above goes by the title *Nine Moon Marvel*. As you can see, it's a static image that has an animated effect. If you don't see the effect, try staring at the white circle in the center of the image for a couple seconds or try scanning over the entire image. Within a couple of seconds, you should see the circles beginning to rotate in both clockwise and counter clockwise directions. These illusions work due to rapid eye movements, as well as blinking.

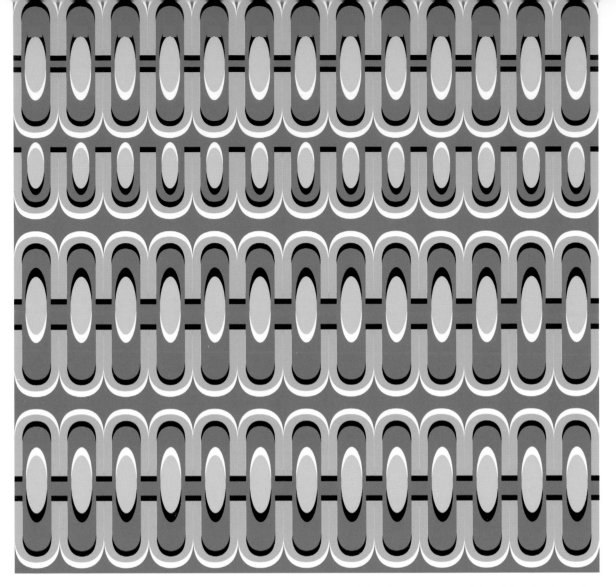

Roller Coaster Wave

The above illusion is titled *Roller Coaster Wave* and for good reason. If you scan over the image with your eyes for a few seconds or just stare at the center of the image, you'll be given the illusion that the image is moving like a roller coaster. Illusions like this are effective because of rapid eye movements, known as saccades, and blinking. So, basically, it's your eyes that are playing tricks on you.

Shiny Wheels

The above illusion is titled *Shiny Wheels*. Mark Grenier is a master at creating these illusions that are static images, but they still are able to give off an animated effect. This particular illusion is certainly one of his more vibrant illusions, as it jumps right out at you. This is mostly due to the color selection he used for this particular illusion. Staring at the image for a brief period of time, you'll likely see the circles in the image begin to turn clockwise and counter clockwise, which is the effect Grenier was trying to achieve.

Illusion created by Mark Grenier

Sparkle Spinners

The above illusion has been given the title *Sparkle Spinners*, by the creator himself, Mark Grenier. Without a doubt, this illusion lives up to its name, as there are some sparkles right in the center of this image. If you stare at the sparkles for just a couple seconds, you'll begin to see the surrounding circles spinning in both clockwise and counter clockwise directions. If staring at the center of the image doesn't work for you, you can try scanning over the image with your eyes.

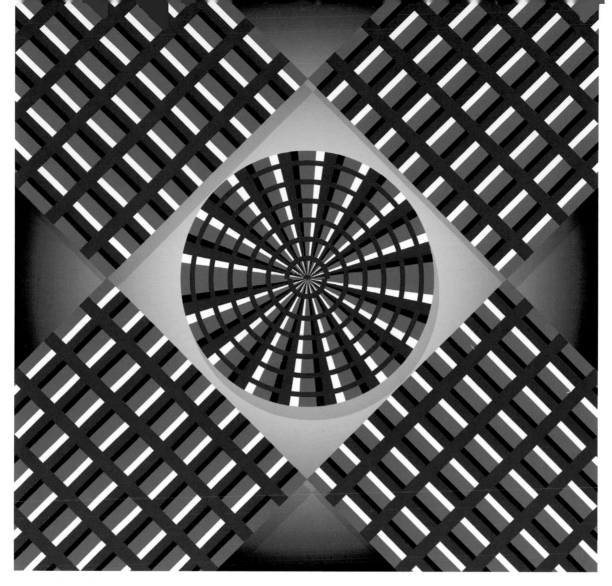

Windmill

The above illusion goes by the title *Windmill*, and for good reason. If you stare at the image for more than a couple seconds, you'll see a windmill effect. If you don't see the effect, try staring at the center of the image for a couple of seconds or scan over the entire image with your eyes.

ZigZag Spinners

ZigZag Spinners is an illusion created by master illusionist Mark Grenier. Mark specializes in creating static images that give off an animated effect. Chances are, this image immediately jumped out at you. The whole image appears to be moving on its own when you look at it. That being said, you're probably wondering how illusions like the one above are created. Well, they use your eyes to power them and give off the desired effect. They rely on rapid eye movements, known as saccades, and blinking.

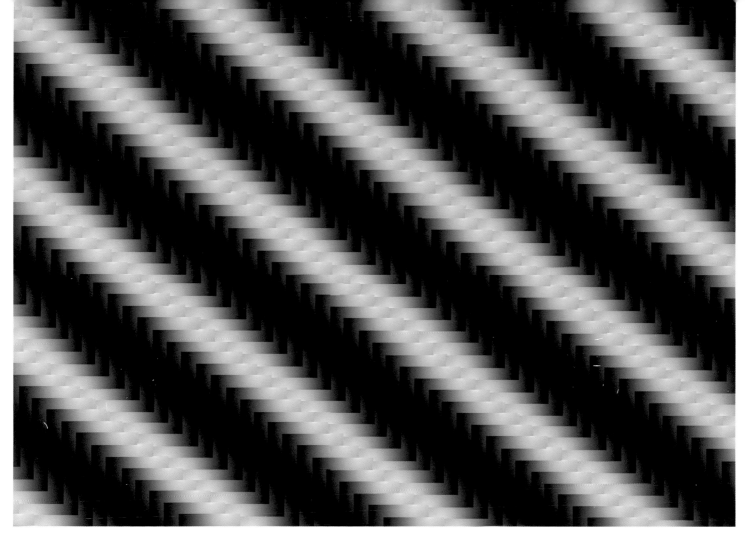

Black and Blue

The above illusion has been dedicated to the father of Richard D. Contreras, as well as his close cousin, Charlie.

The optical illusion above should give off the effect that it's actually moving, despite the fact that the image is completely static. If you don't see the effect, staring at the center of the image for just a couple of seconds should do the trick. The effect looks as if the lines are moving on their own. This illusion works due to rapid eye movements, known as saccades, which give off the moving or "dancing" effect you see above.

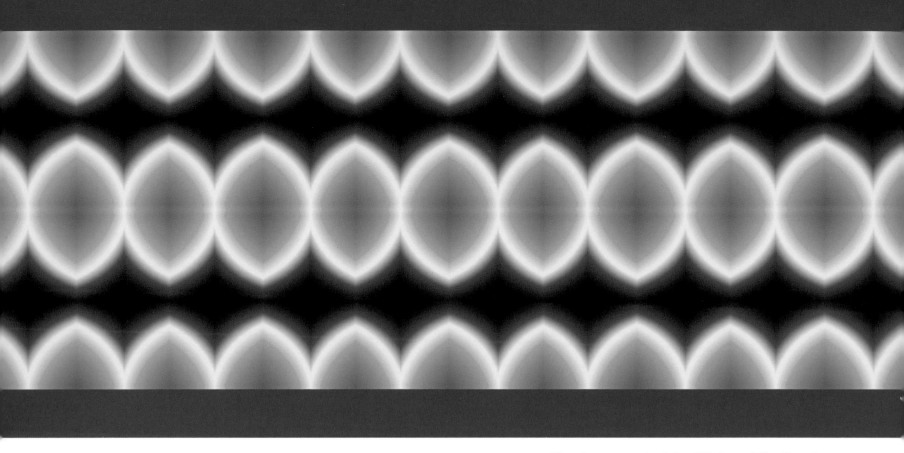

Illusion created by Richard D. Contreras

Expanding Arcs

The above illusion has been dedicated to the father of Richard D. Contreras, as well as his close cousin, Charlie.

Does the illusion in the picture above seem to be moving on its own, despite the fact that it's not animated in any way? It should seem as if the image is expanding, like an opening mouth. If you can't see the effect, you should stare at the center of the image. Try to concentrate on the center of the image, and you should be able to achieve the desired effect.

Wondering how an illusion like this works? Basically, the effect is achieved with rapid eye movements, also known as saccades, as well as blinking. This is just another case of your own eyes playing tricks on you.

Illusion created by Richard D. Contreras

Spinning Sun and More

The above illusion has been dedicated to the father of Richard D. Contreras, as well as his close cousin, Charlie.

There's a bit of confusion surround this illusion, so I'll leave this one up to the viewer. When staring at the center of the image above, do you see the sun spinning or do you actually see the sun pulsating? This illusion has been presented to multiple people with varying reports. Some say the sun is spinning in a circular manner, while others say that the sun seems to pulsate. Ask your friends and family what they see in the image above and then compare the results.

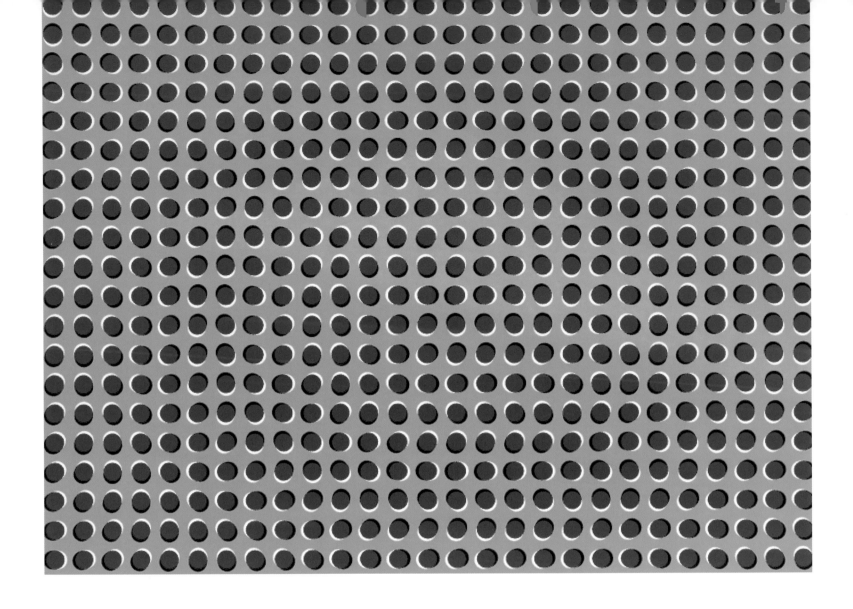

There are some optical illusions that look like they are moving, and a lot of people out there are curious as to how illusions like this are accomplished or how they work. The secret to this really cool optical illusion is the shape of the dots, as well as the combination of both the light and dark undertones. Each one of the little blue dots is outlined half in black, half in white, and the shape of them has a lot to do with how the illusion works, as well.

With something that is partially black and partially white, the eye will have a tendency to follow the white pattern, which is going to make it look like the whole background is moving and that's what gives off the effect you see in the optical illusion above.

Moving optical illusions can be more than just dots, and the above picture is an example of a moving circle. The crescent moons are half black and half white. The human eye is going to follow the white color as it goes from one to another. Another aspect of this optical illusion that makes it appear to move is the fact that there is a smaller inner circle that is also made up of half black and half white crescent moons. The smaller inner circle appears to be moving in the opposite direction, which only helps makes the bigger outer circle look like it, too, is moving.

This is a rather unique illusion because it is a combination of a moving illusion and a 3D illusion in one. For people who are just dying to know how this illusion works, all that they have to do is stare at the direct center of the illusion. Once again, the combination of the black and white in the center, and the blue and yellow on the outer circles, is going to force the human eye to follow the lighter of the two colors.

When people are staring at the middle, and their eyes begin to relax, they are going to start to see the center swirling and popping out of the middle. With the center circle becoming a 3D image, and the light colors on the outer circles, the whole image will begin to start moving around and around.

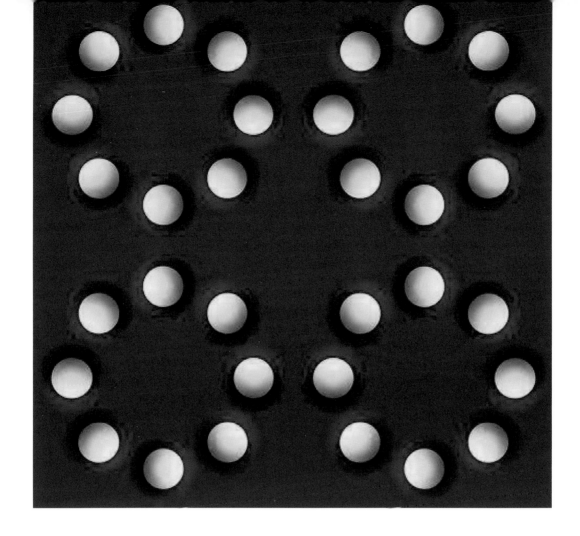

There are colors that are very bright to the human eye, especially when combined with another color. The above optical illusion involves the combination of both purple and yellow. How this illusion is done has to do with the yellow circles. People may notice that there is a shadow around each and every one of those circles. For anyone that has seen the other illusions that are outlined half black and half white, the eye follows the white around, which makes the illusion seem to move.

In the case of this illusion, the shadows are what make this illusion move because the shadows are slightly different for each one of the yellow circles. With this illusion, the eye and brain are going to follow the part of the circle that is not in shadow, which is going to make it look as if every circle is turning and moving together.

The fall means that the leaves on all the trees are changing into the autumn colors of red, brown, yellow, and gold. Not everyone lives in a location that has the trees that change colors, which is why some people end up creating an optical illusion that simulates waving leaves. In order to create the illusion, the first thing a person needs is a bright color that is very eye-catching. Once the background has been created, the next part of the illusion involves the brown almond shapes.

To make the almond shapes appear to be waving like leaves in the wind, each one has been outlined partially in white and partially in black. When all of the images are placed together on the bright green background, the eye and brain will see the whole image appear to be waving.

Anyone that is into any kind of marksmanship recognizes a bull's eye when they see it. The object of the bull's eye is to hit the center and it takes a lot of practice in order to accomplish this goal. The above image is an optical illusion that looks like it is going in a circle before eventually hitting the center. To create this optical illusion, the first thing the creator has to do is pick a bright background that can easily be seen.

Light colors against a dark background are going to capture the eye, especially with the addition of the green right in the middle of the tan arrows that are pointing directly to the center of the image. The lighter points of starburst in the middle of the image is going to make the eyes go around and around before finally going into the center of the bull's eye.

Tornado season happens every spring and it can be quite devastating to some areas of the country. For some people that do not live in what is known as the tornado belt, the only tornados they are exposed to are the kind that are created on a home computer. The above image is a recreated tornado that anyone can do if they know how. The first step to the swirling tornado optical illusion is to get a white background.

In order to create the tornado swirling effect, black squiggly lines have to be added to the white background in the shape of a circle. The black lines are not all the same size, but get progressively smaller as they go toward the middle. As the eyes go around the circle, the white and black combined, plus the shrinking size of the lines, equals the swirling tornado effect.

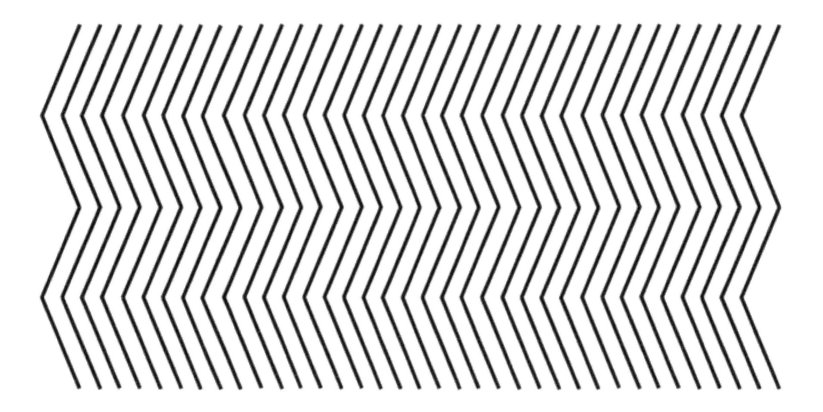

When people see zig zag lines that all look exactly the same, people expect that any optical illusion involving movement would have the lines all moving in the same direction. However, the above optical illusion is a little different. If people stare in the direct center of the image, they will see that the two rows in the middle are moving in the opposite direction sliding along one another. The amazing thing about this optical illusion is the fact that recreating it would not be difficult at all.

For anyone that wants to make this illusion, the directions for it are pretty simple. The zig zag lines are black, and against the white background, the image is going to move all on its own. The combination of the natural function of both the eyes and the brain come together in order for this simple optical illusion to start moving across from one end of the screen to the other.

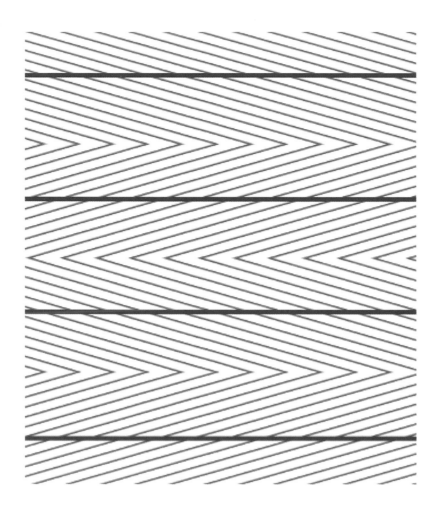

The image above is an optical illusion on more than one level. The white background with the darker lines going in opposite directions appear to be moving because of the combination of light and dark playing a trick on the eyes. However, the addition of the dark lines going across the zig zag lines creates a second optical illusion. The thicker dark lines going across the screen appear to be crooked, but that really is not the case. The combination of the moving zig zag lines, plus the thicker dark lines, makes the straight thicker lines appear to be crooked.

The best way for people to recreate this optical illusion is to use a straight edge of some kind to draw the thick lines across the white background. The secret to the moving zig zags is the fact they are shaped like arrows, which will naturally make the eye see them going in opposite directions.

Anytime anyone sees a circle, people tend to think a record that goes around on a turntable. However, a circle will not move the same way when it is combined with a thick black diamond and a hole in the very center. If people stare directly at the hole in the image, they will see something remarkable. Instead of seeing the circle going around like a record, or like water going down a drain, what is actually moving in the center of the image is a line that appears to be spinning along the circle.

Some people who see the movement in the middle may see a line, or they may also see what appears to be an eight-pointed star. However, whether people take a look at this optical illusion and see the line or the eight-pointed star, they will see the middle of the circle going around and around.

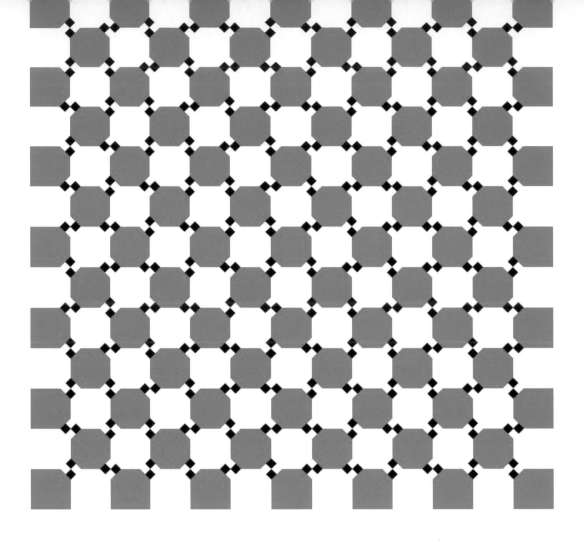

Optical illusions that move usually involve a white or light-colored background. White is the lightest colored there is, which makes it perfect for any kind of moving optical illusion. The above image puts white and green together, but in order to make it move there needs to be something else added to it. Around each of the green dots, there are black and white checkered squares. Each one of the black and white checkered squares has to be placed in a specific way in order to create the movement. Some of the squares are up and down like diamonds, but there are some that are turned to the side.

Because each square is placed in a different way, the eye is going to follow the black squares as they go from one direction to another. If people look from one side of the screen to the other while following the black squares, the whole image will appear to wave like a flag in the breeze.

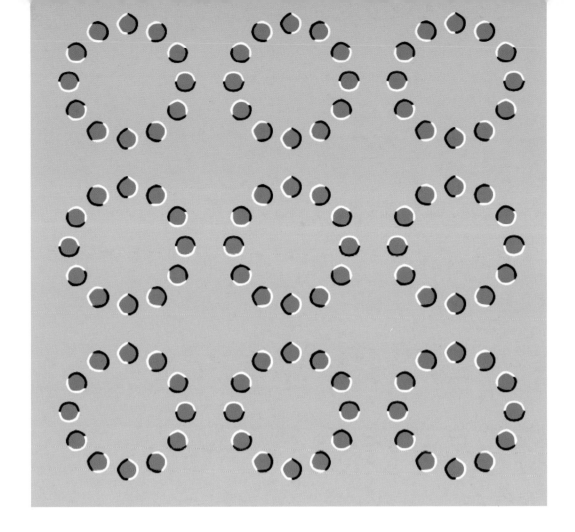

There is something about the color gray that makes people feel very calm. In the image posted above, people are going to see a simple gray background that has nine small gray circles placed upon it. Though the image looks simple, the truth is that it is not because if people look at the gray background long enough, they will notice that the small circles are moving independently.

Each circle is made up of twelve smaller dark gray circles. To make each group of small circles move, people have to look very closely at the smaller dark gray circles. The tiny dark circles are outlined with white on one side and black on the other. To give the appearance of movement, the white line and black line are placed on different sections of the smaller circles.

The above image is very hard on the eyes. When people first look at the black and white circle, they will see that the middle section of it is perfectly clear. However, the longer people stare at the center of the circle, the more they notice that the blurriness on the outside of the circle is beginning to spread. If people stop staring at the middle, moving their eyes from the center, and take a second look, the middle will be clear. The outer circle, slightly out of focus, plays a trick on the eyes and will cause the muscles to strain slightly, which will make the blurriness appear like it is spreading from the outside, working its way to the middle of the circle.

What makes 3D optical illusions a lot of fun is the fact that when people stare at them long enough, the image seems to leap off of the page or screen. The above image is the perfect example of a 3D optical illusion because if people stare at the very center of it long enough, the black and white diagonal lines will begin to rise up and look like pipes.

The diagonal lines are filled in with white and black wavy lines. The eye is going to look at those wavy lines and see where the pipes are being formed because the lines are going to bend around the sides to form the pipes. Also, the fact that the wavy lines go in opposite directions also helps complete the look of the individual pipes when they turn into a 3D image.

Anyone that has ever washed dishes has seen what water looks like as it goes down the drain. The spinning of the water in one direction can be quite hypnotic if people look at it long enough. The above image is an exact recreation of spinning water going down the drain. In order to create the illusion of spinning, people need to stare at the direct center of the circle. The longer the middle is stared at, the more the eyes will relax.

After a few moments, the muscles of the eyes are going to start to go slack, which will make the outer circle start to move. To help make it look like a drain, the white and black lines have a slightly arched end. After that, they start in the center and then work their way out.

The image you see above is a white background with black checkers, but there are also gray checkers that are mixed in. The optical illusion involves the gray squares disappearing right before the eyes. When people first see this image, they may get the mistaken impression that the black squares are going to become a 3D illusion, but that is not the case. When people stare at the center of this image, the grey squares are going to start to vanish.

After about thirty seconds of staring at the image, the black blocks will stand out and the grey blocks will disappear completely. The white and black squares in the middle of the image have no gray around them, which helps make the illusion work.

In deep space, there are phenomena known as black holes. With these black holes, anything and everything gets sucked into it. Black holes are considered to be extremely dangerous because they can devour everything. The truth is that scientists have very little knowledge about black holes except that they are so dangerous that whole planets can get sucked into them and disappear forever.

The image above is a simple checkerboard, but there is a problem with it. On the upper left corner of the checkerboard background, there is a black hole. When people stare at the black hole, something is going to happen to it. The more the black hole is gazed at, the bigger the hole is going to get, making it look like the black and white squares are going to get sucked into it.

Anyone that has ever been out on the ocean may have seen a remarkable event called a whirlpool. The currents in the ocean can go from one direction to another, but at some point, the two might come together to form a swirling whirlpool that can suck down anything and everything it its path, including people and ships. In order to recreate a whirlpool, people need to first create a black and white checkered background. However, with the checkers, they all cannot look the same in order to create the whirlpool effect.

Starting from the second row of checkered squares, they need to start to move from one side to the other. As the viewer looks toward the middle of the image, the squares should become more and more distorted. The squares in the very center of the image should look as close to normal as possible, which will complete the whirlpool illusion.

The ocean is one of the most unexplored places on earth, which just happens to cover more than 70 percent of the planet. There are seven oceans, and little is actually known about these vast spaces filled with very deep water that contains sea life and plant life. The oceans contain currents that move both warm and cold water. There are scientists that spend all of their time studying the flow of the currents to learn more about weather, animal life, and plant life that every ocean contains.

Scientists that specialize in the ocean often have special charts that show the flow of the different ocean currents. For those people that want a really fun illusion, they can recreate the ocean currents by using a black and white checkered background that is going in different directions. When people follow the different checkers, they will appear to be moving just like the ocean currents.

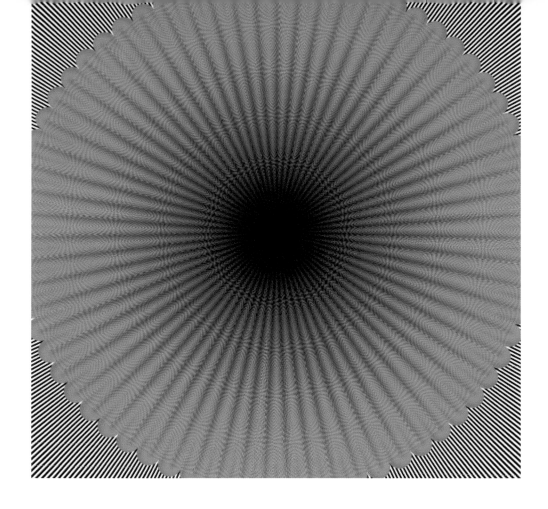

The human eye is a remarkable organ that can take in images that are then translated by the brain so people understand what they are seeing. Without the eyes and the brain working together, no one would be able to see things like different dimensions and optical illusions. In the middle of the eye is the iris, and inside of that is a black area called the pupil.

People can make their own human eye easily using a black and white striped background, a circle using gray curved lines, and a black center. To help the eye to spin, the gray inner circle is made up of curved lines that contain swirling gray circles. When people stare at the black inner circle, the combination of gray curved lines and gray swirling circles gives the illusion of spinning.

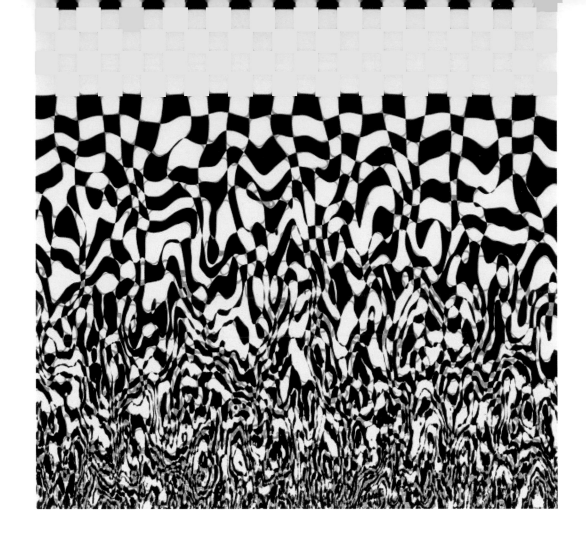

The above picture shows that the sun is so hot that even solid checkerboards made of the strongest materials can melt into a pile of black and white blobs. In order to make a checkerboard background appear to melt, the creator has to start with a half dozen rows of normal-looking checkers. The seventh row of checkers is going to start to show signs of melting, which means that the checkers need to start looking distorted, which changes both the size and shape of the squares.

After the seventh row, the proceeding rows have to look worse and worse until the checkers down toward the bottom are completely ruined. As people look down the melted rows, the two different colors of black and white are going to appear to be sliding and dripping.

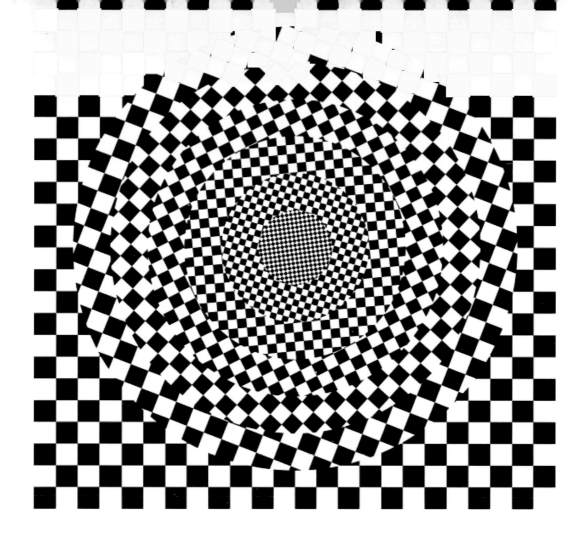

Nothing is more fun than trying to figure out how optical illusions, like the one in the image above, work. The background of the illusion is black and white checkers, but there is also an illusion in the middle that looks like the whole center section is swirling. If people look closely, they will see that the checkers are slowly shrinking from the checkers that are the same size as the ones along the edge, to the very tiny microscopic ones that are in the very center.

There are actually two ways that people can see the swirling center of the optical illusion. People can stare at the direct center of the illusion, and their eyes are going to naturally start looking at every level from the center out. The second way that people can see the swirling motion is to start from the outside and slowly start to look at each level before finally making it to the middle.

When people look at images, like the above black and white checkered image, the first thing they might see is the fact that the image seems to be swirling. However, there is more to this image than swirling black and white checkers that go all around from one side of the picture to the other. One of the most fun things about optical illusions is finding hidden images. The image above is more than just the moving swirls, because there are actually hidden faces among the distorted and misshapen checkers.

There is not an exact number of faces in the above image, but there are also specific parts too. Eyes, noses, and mouths can all be seen in the image above. Give it a shot and see if you can find the hidden faces.

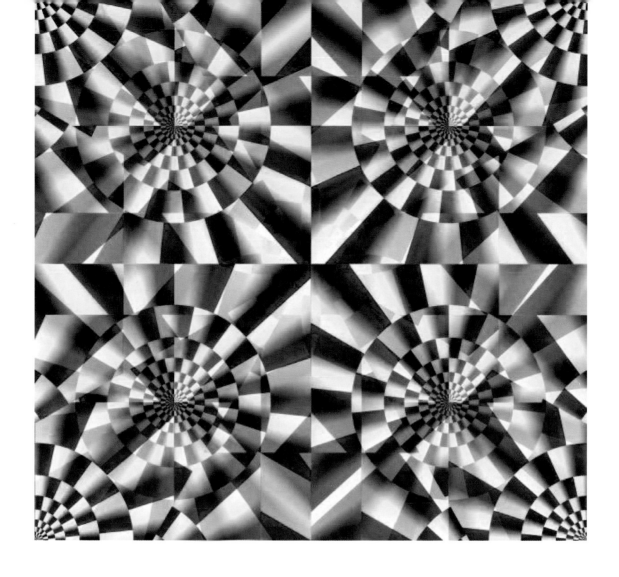

Optical illusions can be made with more than just black and white colors. As long as there is one light and one dark color, any can be used. The above image uses yellow, purple, and pink. The image is divided into four different sections and each one has a wheel in the center. In order to make the wheels in the middle spin, all people have to do is stare directly at the very center where the four squares meet.

After about 30 seconds to one minute, the eyes start to relax, which is going to make each one of the wheels in the center of each square start to spin. What makes this optical illusion really neat is the fact that each circle is moving in the opposite direction.

Pinwheels are available at any store and can provide hours of entertainment for young kids. The above image is a pinwheel image, but this pinwheel is not like those 50 cent pinwheels that people buy for their children. What makes this pinwheel so special is what happens when people stare at the center of it. One thing that may occur when people gaze long enough at this image is that the center may vanish as it starts to spin.

Another thing that may happen is the center may stay, but begin to spin slowly like water going down the drain. Some people may see the lines that are going toward the center start to slowly spin on their own like an airplane propeller. The longer people stare at this image, the more neat things can happen as their eyes relax.

Pinwheels are a lot of fun to play with because they spin around in a circle. If people were to take the time to watch a pinwheel spin, they will notice that sometimes the light makes it look like the wheel is spinning and pulsating. For people who do not have any access to a pinwheel, they can easily recreate this illusion on their own.

The above image is achieved first by getting a background that contains both a light and a dark color. The image in the center of the background is a circle that is surrounded with different layers of light and dark colors. Because the very center circles are eye-catching colors, they are the ones that the eyes will be attracted to.

The above picture is a spinning circle optical illusion that has been created with the colors blue and green. To help make every single circle look like it's spinning, a third color, which is white, has been added in. The trick to this image is to not look at the direct center, but more toward the bottom. Even though the center is not being looked at, the image is going to start to move. The circles in the four corners of the image are also going to move as well, and when they are all moving together, the image is quite an active illusion.

Scary Optical Illusions

Illusion created by Tabi Ferguson

Arm Muscles

Ever wondered what it would be like to see inside of your own arm? Well, makeup FX artist Tabi Ferguson is going to entertain your curiosity. In this image, with a little bit of makeup magic, Tabi has showed us what it would look like if you could see all of the muscles in your forearm. As you can see, the person that the makeup has been applied to has a tattoo on their forearm. I guess this is one very creative way to cover up a tattoo.

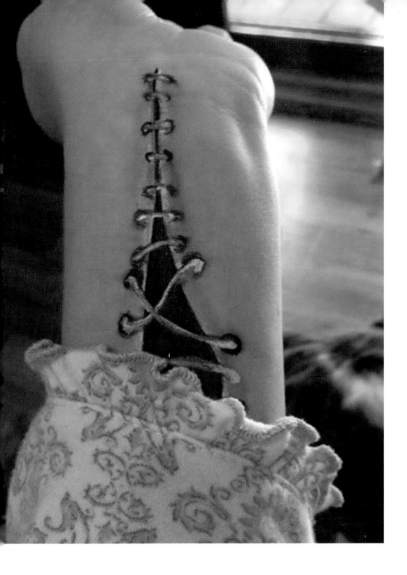

Illusions created by Tabi Ferguson

Arm Stitches

This is very similar to the zipper effect, which has become very popular over the years. Chances are, if you've been to a Halloween store, you've probably seen kits that will enable you to create the zipper effect on your own, which usually gives off the illusion that someone is unzipping their own skin, usually around the facial area, to reveal their insides. Tabi has created a similar effect in this image, but with her own little unique spin. In this image, it looks like someone has had stitches applied to their forearm, but the stitches are coming apart and you can see the insides of the model's arm.

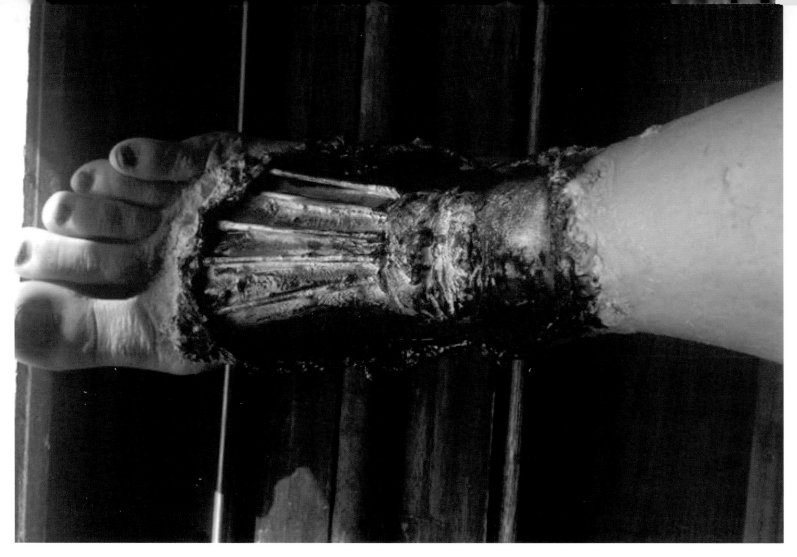

Illusions created by Tabi Ferguson

Foot

This illusion created by Tabi Ferguson looks like it came right out of a horror film. With a little bit of liquid latex and some paint, Tabi was able to create the amazing effect that you see in the image above. It looks as if you can see the inside of someone's foot in the picture. Typically, Tabi likes to show off the muscles when doing effects like this, but this time she takes things a step further and shows us the bones. This certainly is not an illusion that you would want to show to anyone that's squeamish in the slightest bit.

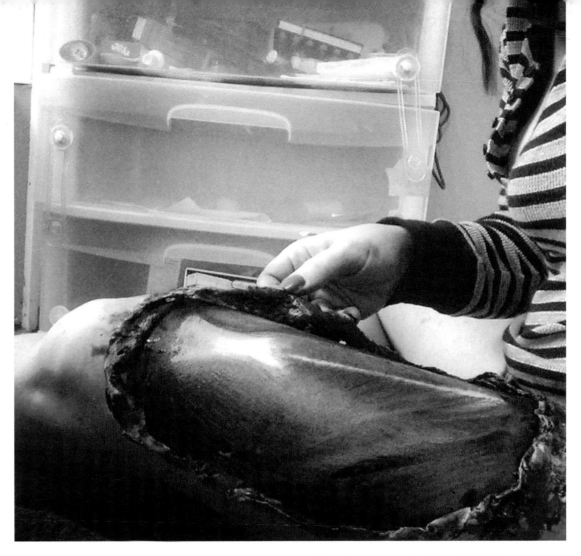

Illusion created by Tabi Ferguson

Leg

Makeup FX artist, Tabi Ferguson, is a master when it comes to manipulating liquid latex and professional grade makeups and paint to get the results that she desires. In this image, we can see what appears to be the inside of someone's thigh. Instead of just using body paint, she used liquid latex to give the effect a bit of depth to make it look as if someone's thigh has actually been torn open. To add to the effect, Tabi is pulling back on the latex, which looks like her own skin, to show off the inside of the leg. With an illusion like this on your body, you'd have no problem being the winner of any costume contest.

Illusion created by Tabi Ferguson

Spider

Typically, master makeup FX artist Tabi Ferguson will use a combination of liquid latex and her masterful painting/makeup skills to create an amazing 3D optical illusion. However, in this particular image, she decided to achieve a scary 3D effect using professional grade paint. In this image, you'll see that it truly looks as if there's a huge spider crawling on Tabi's arm. This would certainly be a very scary effect for anyone that suffers from arachnophobia.